Dear Daddies, Dear Daughters,

*Breaking free from the chains of dysfunction
and finding strength to rewrite our stories*

a memoir

MELINDA JONES

Dear Daddies, Dear Daughters

© 2026 Melinda Jones

ISBN: 979-8-218-89699-7

Table of Contents

*D*ear Daddies,
Dear Daughters,

"For I am persuaded, that neither death, nor life, nor angels, nor principalities, nor powers, nor things present, nor things to come, nor height, nor depth, nor any other creature, shall be able to separate us from the love of God, which is in Christ Jesus our Lord." **Romans 8:38, 39 (KJV)**

"Be not deceived; God is not mocked: for whatsoever a man soweth, that shall he also reap."

Galatians 6:7 (KJV)

Dear Dad's,

Before you dive into these pages, I need you to hear this; you matter more than you know.

Not just as a provider. Not just as a name on the birth certificate.

But as a voice. A protector. A mirror. A presence. A place of safety.

This book is filled with pieces of my story— some funny, some painful, all real. And some are still carrying the weight of what was never said, never shown, never healed.

But it's not too late.

Whether your daughter is 6, 16, or 60—your presence still has power.

So read these words with an open heart. Let them challenge you, comfort you, even convict you if they need to.

Because a daughter who knows her father sees her. Values her and loves her.
That girl walks different. She thinks different. She believes different.

With grace and truth

Preface

The inspiration that got the wheels turning for this long overdue memoir came when I finally sat alone with myself and took a deep, honest look at my life—especially the intimate relationships I'd been in over the years and how they've impacted me, both for better and for worse. During this little revelatory sit-down with myself, I realized there were patterns I had been following without even knowing it. These patterns didn't just pop up out of nowhere—they were rooted in my environment, planted early on, and carefully cultivated over the years by my very first teachers—my mother and father.

Their relationship shaped how I viewed and understood love between a man and a woman—no matter how dysfunctional it may have been. It was my first real-life classroom, and who was the head teacher? My Dad. He was the first man who was supposed to show me what a man should be—first to his wife, my mom, and then to the daughters and sons that came from their union.

I needed my dad more than he'll probably ever know or admit. And it's for that very reason I share my story—because daughters who grow up without their father's presence, love, and attention, it leaves marks. Sometimes deep ones.

So, to all the girls out there—young or grown—who've ever yearned for the love, attention, and upbringing of a caring, present dad, I hope you find it in your heart to forgive. Just know, our dads did the best they could with what they knew—with what they had. They weren't perfect, but they were *our* DADDIES.

1

"IN THE BEGINNING"

Where it all Began

I grew up in a two-parent home in a small town of Jasper County, Mississippi, called Paulding. Up until my adolescent years, I thought my parents' union was okay, being that I knew nothing at such a young age about relationships. Why should that have mattered when the only thing I was concerned with at that time was playing and just being a kid. However, I learned a lot from my parents and how their relationship has played a pivotal role in the relationships I've found myself in throughout my teenage and adult life. Parents be warned; children are always watching and listening even when you think they're not.

It never really clicked until some years ago when I had a full-blown *lightbulb* moment about the repeated disasters—I mean, patterns—in my relationships. Of the three relationships I'll be spilling the tea on in this story, two of them felt like I was fighting in an *escape room*—except there were no clues, no teamwork, and definitely no prize at the end.

One day, I was lying on my bed, lost in deep thought (or maybe just avoiding laundry, who knows), wondering what I *could* have done differently—if only I had the wisdom back then that I do now. And just like that, *bam!* It hit me like a ton of bricks: everything I thought I knew about relationships had been downloaded straight from my childhood.

From adolescence to my teen years, I was basically running on autopilot, mimicking what I saw my parents do—completely unaware that I was following a script I never actually signed up for. That was my **"Ah-ha!"** moment, the realization that had me staring at the ceiling and asking myself, *Have I ever even witnessed a real, healthy relationship?* The answer shot back just as fast as the question entered my brain: *Momo and Pawpaw.* My grandparents were the only two people who actually *modeled* what love, partnership, and mutual respect should look like. Turns out, they were the relationship goals I never knew I had!

I was only around seven or eight years old but I knew they loved and cared for one another. Momo and Pawpaw were in their late sixties, and I enjoyed every minute with them. My grandparents were considered middle-class during this time. Momo was a retired elementary school teacher. I'm not sure what Paw-paw's line of work was, but they both were the only black business owners in the area. They ran a small grocer and gas station called Jones Grocery.

My sister Teresa and I *loved* spending time at the store with Momo and Pawpaw. We were basically weekend regulars—hanging out, helping out, and soaking up all the love (and snacks). Momo actually taught us how to read before we even started school, so yeah, she was kind of a big deal. We weren't just there to chill—we had jobs! We'd grab items for customers, bag things up, and every now and then, Pawpaw would let us work the register like we were mini cashiers-in-training. He'd teach us how to count money, and honestly, we felt like total pros. Those moments with them? They are still some of my absolute favorites. I miss them like crazy. The way Momo and Pawpaw were with each other, you didn't need a long speech to understand their relationship—it was just *there*, plain as day. They did everything together. They watched TV together and even went to bed at the same time—it was all part of their rhythm. They had this quiet, unshakable kind of love that didn't need words to be felt. And that connection, it was so real, so deep, that even in passing, they couldn't bear to be apart for long. When they left this world, it was less than thirty days apart—because where one went, the other was sure to follow.

I believe they are in heaven enjoying each other's company as they had done for years together on earth.

As I thought about and reflected on my grandparents' relationship as I had seen as a little girl, I began to wonder how in the hell did my mom end up with someone like my dad when she had the perfect upbringing? In my quest for answers, I came to realize that my mom's past left a pretty deep hole in her heart—one that only God can really fill, and questions only He can truly answer. Honestly, she's a product of what she went through growing up, shaped by things that were way out of her control.

Her childhood? Let's just say it was *complicated*. My mom was born into a situation that was messy from the start. She was conceived by two people who were both married... just not to *each other*. Yep—adultery is how she ended up in this world. Not exactly the warmest welcome, right?

My mom doesn't like speaking about her childhood much because she only knows what she knows, which isn't a whole lot. We both found out a few things a few years ago when I was getting my master's degree in school counseling. One of my assignments was to create a genogram (basically a family tree on steroids), and that's when I stumbled upon something unexpected—turns out, my mom was actually adopted by one of Pawpaw's brothers instead of Momo and Pawpaw themselves. Legally, she belonged to someone else, but in reality, Momo and Pawpaw were the ones who raised her.

When we both heard this, her reaction was just as shocked as mine. Neither of us saw that coming. There was *so much* about her childhood that had been neatly swept under the rug, and now, it all made sense. No wonder she gets uncomfortable whenever I try to joke around or casually bring up the past—because for her, it's not just old family stories. It's a whole lot of *complicated.*

My mom was sent to live with Pawpaw's sister after being scalded with coffee at the hands of her mom's husband, who was not her biological father. Remember that ugly word ADULTERY. My mom's exact age is unknown, but she was a young baby when this awful thing happened to her. Afterward, she was sent to live with Momo and Pawpaw, my grandparents, the brother and sister-in-law of my mother's biological father. She remained there and was reared in a loving and caring household until she met and married my father after finishing high school and after rescinding her full scholarship in music at Rust College.

My mom has a lot of unanswered questions about her childhood—things she may never get the full story on. I try to remind her, though, that even with all the unknowns, her life ended up being better than it probably would've been if her biological mom had raised her. Sometimes, the way things *don't* work out is actually a blessing. She was placed in the care of loving individuals, and she never was in want of anything. Who knows how life would have been for her had she remained in an environment where she was not the legitimate child of her mother's current husband. Mom just responds by saying, "Yeah I know." However, deep down I know she wants more answers than the small assurance that I am offering to try and ease her pain from all this. One question in particular that weighs heavily on her mind is why her mom gave her away and not her other siblings. My mom is the second born of five children of her mom. She was the only one sent away to live with her biological father's brother.

You might be wondering, *Well, why didn't her biological dad just raise her himself?* Great question. Here's the thing—he was already *very much* married with a whole family of his own. And back in those days, bringing home an illegitimate baby to your wife and kids was basically the social equivalent of showing up to a black-tie event in a clown suit. Not a good look.

Funny (well, not *haha* funny), but it kinda mirrors how my mom felt when *my* dad showed up with his own surprise baby and dropped it into our household like it was no big deal. According to my mom, the day she was born, her biological dad packed up his entire family and *moved to another state.* Like... *poof!* Problem solved. Can you imagine?

Now seriously, think about that—finding out you were conceived through an affair, and *neither* parent stuck around? That kind of truth hits hard. I'm sure the way she felt isn't too far off from what a lot of kids in foster care experience. Because at the end of the day, nobody wants to feel like the afterthought of their own origin story.

My mom has managed to keep in contact from time to time with siblings from both sides of her parents; however, calls are few, far, and in between I'm told.

What I remember about my mom's biological parents is that there was always a sense of distance—not just in miles, but emotionally, too. Her father had moved up to Pennsylvania with his second wife, building a new life there, while her mother was still in Mississippi, less than an hour away, but not really present. Even though they weren't far apart geographically, it always felt like there was a bigger gap between them—one that couldn't be measured in just miles.

Granny would visit us every now and then, sometimes for a weekend, sometimes for a whole week. And let me tell you, during those visits, Teresa and I got to see a *very* different side of her—one we never even knew existed.

It turns out, Granny could *throw down* when it came to drinking. I mean, I had to do a double take when she got *pissy drunk* at a baseball game down the road and had to be *delivered* back to our house like an Amazon package gone wrong. Mom had mentioned that Granny liked to drink, but I don't think even she expected her to get so wasted that she'd *pass out, wet her pants,* and need a full-on recovery period at our house.

By the time she sobered up and was back to the sweet, familiar Granny we knew, I couldn't help but wonder, *Did she even remember what happened? Did she feel embarrassed? Did she feel ashamed of what we had witnessed in her drunken state?*

I never looked forward to her visits, especially when she came and stayed for an entire week. That meant she was going to be asking questions and bossing me around. You see, I was a lazy kid who enjoyed sleeping in on the weekends and finding ways to get out of doing chores.

My dad would come into our room on a day that I'd decided to sleep in and say, "You think it's your birthday? Get your ass up."

I couldn't stand having my sleep cut short and having to leave the comfort of my bed when I wasn't ready, especially when it was the weekend or during the summer months when school was out.

When Granny would come, she would ask my mom, "Why don't you make Linda get up and help Teresa?"

I wished she would mind her own business. I would mumble under my breath, but my mom would make me get up and help my sister clean the house, which seemed to be a daily thing. There was always something to do around the house no matter how many times we'd clean. I used to say that my parents only had children, so they could have their own personal live-in slaves. I had never seen two lazy parents in my life. My mom wasn't working at the time and was home all day, but she would make Teresa and I clean the house as soon as we got home from being up at 6 a.m. for school, spending all day there getting an education and arriving home to do more work. But here's the real kicker. Mom *hated* making cornbread—like, with a passion. And in the South, where cornbread is practically a food group, that meant she passed the duty down to me or Teresa. Every. Single. Time.

Teresa and I had a solid game plan to avoid getting stuck with cornbread duty: we'd hide in our room, wedged between the wall and the bed, completely covered in blankets like two little fugitives on the run. The goal? Stay invisible long enough to sneak in a nap before Mom could find us.

It was working *beautifully*—until I went and ruined it. One day, Teresa called first dibs, meaning *I* had to make the cornbread. In my frustration (and sheer pettiness), I let our secret hiding spot slip. Just like that, *boom*—our foolproof escape plan was dead, and neither of us could use it again. I thought I was fixing *her*—turns out, I just ruined it for *both* of us. A classic rookie mistake.

To put it nicely, Mom was fully enjoying the *sweet, sweet* revenge of making us pay for every ounce of labor pain we ever put her through. And how did she do it? By assigning us *chores*—specifically the ones she *easily* could have done while we were at school but *chose* to save for us.

What could we do about it? Absolutely *nothing*. Unless, of course, you were feeling bold enough to test your luck—which, in our house, meant risking an ass-whooping. And let me tell you, those came around just as frequently as our *mandatory* cornbread-making shifts. It was like clockwork: clean, cook, dodge an ass-whooping—repeat.

To this very day, Teresa and I hate making cornbread because we had to make it so much when we were teens. Today, we all laugh and make jokes about it with my mom and she just gives us this look as if our perspective of it is all wrong and distorted. Getting back to Granny, I did not enjoy her visits because she interfered with my sleep and laziness. As I got older, her visits became less, to non-existent. Granny was older now and had matured beyond her days of drinking heavily as I remembered and had accepted Jehovah into her life. During her last visit, she seemed more poised, but she still had that urge to tell you what to do. However, I did as she said without a mumbling word.

During the development of my genogram, I learned that Granny had been married four times and her children were a product of those marriages, excluding my mom. Although Granny did not send her other children away to live with someone else, they were raised by someone other than herself, an aunt. Mom had a longing to be close to her sisters and brothers and it bothered her deeply.

"If you didn't want her, you should've left her where she was!" That's what Pawpaw snapped at my dad one hot, sticky summer day as we all stood awkwardly in the doorway of the den in our mobile home.

I was probably around eleven or twelve—old enough to know *drama* when I saw it. I just stood there thinking, *Is this real life?* Yep. It was all going down, live and unfiltered, right in front of me. No commercials. No warning. Just pure, front-row family chaos.

Hearing of my dad's infidelity must have weighed heavily on Pawpaw for him to come to the house to confront Daddy. Already advanced in age, Pawpaw walked with a cane and moved very slowly as if each step he made was in slow motion. I remember the look on my daddy's face as Pawpaw spoke those words. My dad was a mean and surly man, at least to me and my siblings and mom. To tell you the truth, I hated my dad growing up. Daddy stood reserved and quiet as Pawpaw came to his daughter's aid.

You're probably wondering how Pawpaw found out about Daddy's little side adventure, right? Well, buckle up, because here's how it all went down. Teresa—my sister and the *undisputed queen* of eavesdropping. She had a PhD in listening to grown folks' business. It was so bad, we nicknamed her "Growny-Rony" because she was always posted up somewhere, silently absorbing every juicy adult conversation like a sponge with ears.

Any time we were at Grandma's house (aka the headquarters for grown-up gossip), and my dad caught Teresa lurking nearby with that *I-heard-every-word* look on her face, he'd snap, "Get your ass outside and play!" Of course, she'd act like she *just happened* to be standing there—but we all knew better.

And yes, it was *Teresa the Ear-Hustler* who let the cat out of the bag and spilled the beans to Pawpaw about Daddy's affair. I shouldn't have laughed, but I did. Because honestly, if anyone was going to blow up the family secrets, it was definitely going to be her.

This was the *one*-time Teresa and I weren't told, "Get your asses outside and play." Nope—we had front-row seats to the drama, and trust me, it was better than any soap opera. I bet Daddy was silently wishing he could teleport *anywhere* else—Mars, a cave, the neighbor's doghouse—just *not* where he was standing. The look on his face? Pure gold. Like a deer in headlights thinking, *Is this actually happening right now?*

I've always been a bit of a jokester—never one to pass up a chance for a good laugh. And if I'd had the nerve in that moment (which, let's be real, I probably did), I would've looked him dead in the eye and said, "Hell yes, this is happening—and good for your cheating ass!"

Let's just say, out of the five of us kids, I was definitely the loud one, the *mouthy* one, and the one who didn't mind saying what everyone else was thinking. And if you stick around, you'll see exactly what I mean.

I'm not exactly sure what pushed Teresa to spill the tea on Daddy, but I'd like to believe it came from a place of love and concern for Mama—or maybe she just hit her daily drama quota early. Either way, once it was all out in the open, I *know* she regretted opening her mouth. As soon as Pawpaw left and got back home, Daddy turned into a full-blown detective, pacing the house like he was on *CSI: Family Edition*, grilling everyone with that "somebody's gonna pay" energy. And when he found out it was Teresa? Whew, he was *mad, mad.* He gave her the kind of whooping that made you rethink every life choice you've ever made. Isn't it funny how parents seem to think that a whooping was the remedy for everything you did wrong? I wished there were counselors around back then, because my parents could have used some advice like, *Why don't you just talk to your child and tell them what was wrong about what they did instead of beating them?* Knowing my dad, he probably would have beaten the counselor for coming to him with that bullshit. I could hear him now saying in his southern drawl, "You betta git yo ass away from here with that goddamn shit."

I felt sorry for her, but I was kind of glad she told Pawpaw because I had seen Mama sad and crying because of my dad's infidelity. I hated seeing mom upset, which seemed to be often because she was treated like she was the other woman while that homewrecker was embraced by his side of the family like she was the wife. Here's the caveat. My dad ended up having a child with her.

I have never acknowledged his outside child as my sister, and I have my reasons, thanks to my dad. He treated the five of us—his kids with my mom—like we were nothing, always cursing us out and saying, "Y'all ain't shit. You motherfuckers ain't ever gonna be shit." He inflicted on us all kinds of verbal abuse but not that bastard child he conceived with the other woman. He treated her like she was royalty, no joke. I remember it like it was yesterday—I needed a few bucks, maybe five- or ten-dollars tops, and I asked Daddy for it.

He snapped back with all the attitude in the world, "I ain't got no money."

Cool. Got it. But later that same day, I watched from my parents' bedroom window as he reached into his back pocket, pulled out his wallet, and handed *her* money like it was nothing. That moment hit me hard. I hated him even more after that. And as for his outside kid, yeah, I never liked or cared for her—and that day just sealed the deal on how I felt about both of them.

I can't help but remember all the hurtful names and things my siblings and I were called by our dad. His words stuck with us and left scars that still linger today. But the outside child, she never got that treatment.

Still, despite everything he said about us, we all went on to do well—we earned degrees, built successful careers, and proved him wrong in every way. The same things he said we'd never be? That's exactly what *she* became.

It's funny how God works though. He took what was meant to tear us down and used it to lift us up. *"You intended to harm me, but God intended it for good, to accomplish what is now being done"* **Genesis 50:20 (NIV).**

I'm not sure if I will ever get over how I feel about my dad's outside child, and it's not her fault that she's a product of what her mom and my dad did, but that's just something God will have to continue to help me with.

"Why won't you just leave him?" I asked Mom one day, standing at the foot of her bed while she was clearly fed up with Dad's latest shenanigans. I was genuinely trying to understand. "Do you even love him?" I followed up, curious.

Before she could say a word, I—being the dramatic little truth-teller I was—blurted out, "Well, *I* hate him!"

Whew. Big mistake. HUGE. Mama moved so fast, you'd think someone lit a fire under her. In a flash, she grabbed a switch like she was pulling a sword from a holster and proceeded to whoop my ass like I had personally offended her ancestors. She beat me so good for saying I hated my dad, the word *hate* got permanently deleted from my vocabulary. To this day, even if someone lies, steals, or eats the last slice of cake I was saving, I still won't say I hate them. I'll just say, "I strongly dislike them with the fire of a thousand suns," and keep it pushing.

Just so we're clear—after that whooping, I *never* asked Mom another question about why she stayed with Dad. That mystery remained unsolved— and unspoken.

For the longest time, I just couldn't figure out why my mom didn't leave him. I mean—he had *nothing*. Like, absolutely nothing. No savings, no backup plan, no legacy to leave behind. Meanwhile, Momo and Pawpaw had done right by their daughter, my mom, and made sure she had something to fall back on. But my dad, he came from nothing, wanted nothing, and honestly did a whole lot of *nothing*—except treat us all like crap. So, I chalked it up to love. She must've loved him too much to leave. What else could it be?

But there was a bigger question that haunted me, *Why didn't he leave her—and us—and go be with the other woman?* I've never asked. And after all these years, I'm not about to open that can of worms.

If I had to guess, though? He probably stayed because he had more to lose than gain by walking away. He didn't have much, and neither did the other woman, so he stayed right where the benefits were—on the land he farmed, with food on the table and some kind of stability. That whole "have your cake and eat it too" thing? Oh, he *ate*. Trust me.

It wasn't until years later, when I found myself in a similar situation, that I finally got it. I stayed, too. Just like my mom did. It turned out, I'd been watching, listening, and learning from them all along—whether I realized it or not. It was a pattern, one I didn't even know I was repeating until I was smack in the middle of it. It wasn't until my sister and I became young adults that I realized just how screwed up my parent's relationship was concerning his infidelity. The plot thickens.

After our grandparents passed on to glory (probably up there shaking their heads), the "good life" as we knew it packed its bags and left with them. My dad was no longer providing for his immediate family because he was trying to take care of two households. Either one will have and the other will lack. You guessed it! We lacked in every sense of the word. With our grandparents gone and the chance of having anything decent—food, clothing, and basic necessities were long gone, and we were up shits creek without a paddle most days. We went from name-brand food items to no-frills at the grocery store. When it came to clothing, I remember having only two pairs of shoes that were shared with my sister. We had a pair of high-top Converse sneakers and a pair of blue penny loafers. We didn't have much in clothing as well. If my sister wore a pair of jeans one day, I would wait a day or two and wear those same jeans unwashed, ironed, and smelling of the dirt she had left on them from when she wore them. This was the norm. Every school year mom would go to a store in a nearby town and get us school clothes on a five-hundred-dollar credit my dad had her apply for, so we could have clothes for the beginning of the school year.

Just when I thought things couldn't possibly get any worse, we downgraded from a few sad-bags of no-name groceries to one or two *tiny* boxes of food from some dusty little mom-and-pop store that looked like it sold both groceries *and* tractor parts. We always looked forward to when Daddy would decide to put food in the house. That box would show up like it was some kind of prized delivery. That giant block of cheese wrapped in that thick red plastic (you needed a chainsaw to cut it), a roll of bologna the size of a small log, a rainbow of random Kool-Aid packets, a bag of sugar, a loaf of bread, and a few other items. As soon as food entered, it went just as quickly. Seven mouths had to be fed, and five of them belonged to young, growing kids. There were three girls and two boys—one of whom acted like he was starving *all the damn time.*

My dad had what most people would call a good job with what I *guess* was decent pay back then. He worked for Shell Oil Company. We lived in a big double-wide mobile home with central air and heat, which basically made us middle-class royalty in our little world. From the outside, folks probably thought we were doing just fine. But if only they knew. My siblings and I rarely had any money—not even a little pocket change for school. And asking Dad. Oh, please. He wasn't giving us a single penny unless we *earned* it. And even then, by the time he finished cussing us out and calling us every name in the book (especially some version of "bastard"), it wasn't even worth the emotional damage we had to take just to walk away with two or three bucks.

I remember every payday like clockwork—Dad would come home already mad, like he preheated his attitude on the drive over, just to make sure nobody (including Mom) dared to ask him for money. It was his way of saying, "Don't even think about it" without actually saying it. But me, I secretly *loved* payday weekends. Because while he thought he was the only one getting paid, I had my own little side hustle going. What he didn't hand over while sober, I quietly collected during his "drunk and knocked out" phase. I'm not exactly proud of it. But listen, desperate times called for sneaky measures. He left me no choice—and honestly, in my mind, it wasn't stealing. It was reimbursement. Back pay, if you will. As far as I was concerned, he *owed* me and Teresa. I was just cashing in. So, I considered we were even.

My dad didn't stop his cheating ways with just his main side chick—oh no, he kept the drama going like it was a full-time job. But here's where it really gets wild. Teresa and I used to *spend the night* at this woman's apartment from time to time, and Mom was *totally cool* with it. Like, no big deal. And the part that still blows my mind, I remember this one night clear as day—my dad, my *mom,* and *his other woman* all went out clubbing together. Yep. The three of them, just out on the town like it was girls' night plus Dad.

These days, my siblings and I just look back, shake our heads, and ask ourselves, "What the hell were our parents thinking?" Especially Mom. Like seriously, was this normal to them? Because to us, it was straight-up sitcom-level chaos.

Why did she accept my dad's infidelity—and even *tolerate* (for lack of a better word) the woman who helped wreck her marriage and our family? Was she just tired of feeling less than? Tired of feeling unwanted? What made her stay and put up with the emotional mess and abuse?

Mom is now seventy-three and battling cancer. My hope is to sit down with her—while she's still able to talk and share—and ask her these questions before I finish this book. I want to understand where her head and heart were during all of it. I want to know what it felt like to constantly have to compete for the love, affection, and loyalty that should've been hers as a wife—no questions asked.

2
"A DREAM"

Not all girls dream of fairy tale weddings,
kids and homes with white picket fences—some
dream only of escaping the nightmare.

The year was 1988, and I was *thrilled* to finally be in my senior year of high school. I had made it to the finish line—and let me tell you, college or a career was nowhere on my radar. Not even a blip. I wasn't one of those kids with a five-year plan or a dream school in mind. Nope. I've always had a long list of things I wanted to do and wasn't about to be boxed in by one boring path. Why limit myself when the world was basically a giant sampler platter, and I was ready to try *everything*?

At one point, I wanted to be tall enough to model. Did I have the height? Nope. Did I think I was pretty enough? Also, nope. But that didn't stop me from daydreaming like I was about to be the next Naomi Campbell... just, you know, in a fun-size version.

Then, I thought maybe I'd join the military. That lasted about as long as it took me to realize I don't like being yelled at. After that, I moved on to

Melinda Jones

wanting to be an anesthesiologist, which sounded cool until I realized I'd probably have to *like* science and stay in school forever.

I wanted to be *all these things*, but I never settled on just one. My main goal at that point? Make it to the end of senior year without losing my mind. My indecisiveness about life after high school probably had something to do with the fact that I didn't really have any role models—well, except my grandma, the schoolteacher (shoutout to her for holding it down). Career guidance? Yeah, that wasn't exactly pouring in from my school counselor or any of my teachers. They weren't exactly shouting "Go be great!" from the rooftops. It was more like a shrug and a "Good luck out there." But honestly, none of my dreams or "maybe-I'll-do-this" plans held a candle to my number one ambition: *getting the hell away from my parents and their tyrannical rule.* That was the real goal. I knew deep down I wasn't meant to stay in Mississippi forever. I truly believed if I stuck around and just… settled? It would've killed me—*figuratively*, of course (but still, yikes).

I always felt like a big fish floating in a stream—not a pond. And let me break that down: in a stream, there's movement, a way forward. But life in Mississippi felt so slow, so repetitive, like every day was a rerun. People settled into it like an old recliner, and maybe that was fine *for them*, but it wasn't going to work for me. My dreams were too loud, my ambition too stubborn, and I had zero interest in staying stuck in a place that felt like it had *nothing* to offer me. My role models—Momo and Pawpaw—were gone, and with them went my built-in life compass. So, now I was sitting there like, *Okay…now who am I supposed to look up to?* The answer? Crickets.

Let's go back to that fish analogy for a sec. In a pond, sure, you've got a little wiggle room. You can swim over here or over there, but no matter where you go—it's still the same ol' pond water. That's how I felt about Mississippi. No matter what part of the state you were in, it all felt the same: slow, stale,

26

and predictable. And the idea of moving to another part of Mississippi? *Absolutely not.* The thought didn't even get the chance to form before my brain hit it with a "girl, please."

It felt like living inside one of those small-town movies where people wake up, clock into a factory or some local clinic, go home, rinse, repeat—then hit rewind on the weekend. Saturday? Grocery shopping. Sunday? Church. And then boom—back to Monday like clockwork. *Every. Single. Week.* That life might've worked for other folks but not me. My eyes were set on something bigger—a new city, a new state, somewhere with lights, opportunity, and a *little bit of chaos,* please and thank you. Leaving Mississippi wasn't just a dream—it was *the* mission. And I was gonna make it happen, by any means necessary.

I was seventeen when I made the *official* decision to leave Mississippi—and I mean *leave.* No plan, no strategy, and not even a dollar to my name. I didn't know *how* I was going to go. I just knew I *was.* The mindset was simple: I'm out, and the only thing that could stop me was death. Dramatic? Maybe. But I meant it.

I remember boldly writing in my high school yearbook that I'd end up in either New York or Los Angeles. LA seemed like the obvious choice—I had a whole squad of family out there who had already escaped the Mississippi slow lane in search of something better. But surprise, surprise... I landed in *New York.* And let me tell you, I was not ready. New York slapped me with reality really quick. I thought I was walking into a city of lights, fashion, and fabulousness. Instead, I got hit with cold wind, crazy drivers, and people who will bump into you and keep walking like *you* were in their way. "New York, New York, the big city of dreams—but everything in New York ain't always what it seems." I had heard that line in a rap song before and thought, *dang, they really weren't lying.* It was cute in the lyrics—less cute when I was living it!

I remember my best friend at the time telling me about this place called Whitney M. Young Job Corps Center. Her oldest sister was already there and suggested we sign up, too. It didn't take much convincing for me—*any* chance to start my journey into the real world and I was like, "Where do I sign?"

Now, convincing my parents—*aka* mainly my mom—was a whole different situation. My dad? He couldn't have cared less where we went as long as we weren't standing in front of the TV or asking him for anything. But Mom? Whew. She wasn't trying to hear it. Letting me off what felt like the family *plantation* was going to take a miracle.

Even though she wasn't feeling it, I was already mentally packed. The only thing in my way was the fact that I wasn't legally grown yet—because apparently back then, you were still considered a kid until you were basically halfway to retirement. I needed her signature to make it official, and after enough bugging, begging, and probably a little guilt-tripping, she finally gave in and signed the papers. And let me tell you, when she did, I was ready to throw a going-away party for myself, pack my bags and sprint into freedom like I was starring in my own coming-of-age movie. That signature was my ticket to freedom, and I was gone faster than you could say, "Job Corps bound, baby!"

In the days leading up to my big getaway—oops, I mean "departure"—my grandma on my dad's side and my mom tried *really hard* to talk me out of going. According to them, Job Corps was basically where all the "bad kids" went—the ones who dropped out of school, got into fights, or were one wrong move away from a mugshot. I wasn't hearing it. They could've told me Jason, Freddy, *and* Michael Myers were all hanging out at Job Corps, and I still would've been like, "Cool, I'll take my chances." At that point, anywhere that wasn't *home* felt like paradise. I was convinced freedom came in the form of a Greyhound bus ticket, and baby, I was *on it*.

So, there I was, sweating on a Greyhound in the middle of July 1988, heading to Simpsonville, Kentucky like I was going off to live my best life. Spoiler alert: I was not. That one decision ended up steering me straight into a rollercoaster of drama, heartbreak, poor choices, and enough regret to fill a diary—and yet, somehow, it still beat being stuck in Mississippi!

At Whitney M. Young Job Corps Center, I somehow managed to run smack into the *knockoff version* of my dad—like if he came with fewer morals and more attitude. Lucky me, right? Yep, this guy ended up becoming my personal headache, heartache, and full-time abuser for the next several years. It was definitely *not* what I signed up for when I packed my bags thinking I was chasing freedom.

Job Corps wasn't exactly what my family had hyped (or *warned*) it up to be, but I'll give them this—they were right about one thing: it was definitely a place for teens who had dropped out of school for all kinds of reasons and were trying to get their GED. And yes, some of them had *issues*—like real ones. But honestly, don't we all? I had my own suitcase full of emotional baggage, so who was I to judge?

To me, Job Corps was a way out—a much-needed escape from a world that felt way too overwhelming to figure out on my own. It was a place where you could start fresh, get a better sense of who you were (or at least who you didn't want to be), and pick up a life skill or two while you were at it. Basically, it was a make-it-or-waste-it kind of deal, and the ball was definitely in your court.

I met all kinds of people—girls and guys who had been there for *years* and treated the place like it was home. As for me? I had no plans of making it my forever spot. I came in with a mission: pick a trade, stay my six months, and bounce straight into the real world. Preferably with a skill, a plan, and maybe just a little less uncertainty than I started with.

WMYJCC had rules—*real* rules—and they didn't just post them for decoration. They were enforced, and trust me, you knew it. We were up early in the morning, handling whatever assigned detail we had before getting ready for classes in the trade we chose. The place ran a tight ship, and we were expected to pull our weight. In a way, it gave you a little taste of the real world—responsibility, routine, and people in charge who didn't care if you were having a bad hair day.

Before graduating high school, I honestly had no clue what I wanted to do with my life. I didn't even know *who* I was, let alone what I was supposed to be. The idea of "success"—whatever that even meant—never really crossed my mind. I've always believed that success is personal. What it means for one person could look totally different for someone else. Only *you* know what that looks like for you... well, *you and God*, if it fits in His plan.

I wanted to be a lot of things. Like I said before, I was never that person who had one clear dream or goal. My heart wasn't set on one lane—I wanted to explore them all. Why limit myself when there were so many paths calling my name?

Now that I'm older, I still feel the same way. I continue to chase and collect little wins and accolades that feel good in the moment, and then—just like that—I'm on to the next thing. Some people might say that's a crazy way to live. Honestly, I used to agree. For a while, I really thought something was wrong with me. Like, *how could anyone feel successful constantly bouncing from one thing to another?*

Then one day, a colleague introduced me to Elizabeth Gilbert's *Flight of the Hummingbird*, and that changed everything for me. It flipped my whole perspective. For the longest time, I thought something was wrong with me because I didn't have that one blazing passion everyone talks about — that "drop everything and devote your life to it" kind of calling. I've tried different things, loved some, outgrew others, and sometimes felt guilty for changing directions. But Elizabeth Gilbert's words helped me see myself differently. I'm not lost — I'm a hummingbird. I'm meant to move from flower to flower, learning, growing, and carrying pieces of one experience into the next. My path may not be a straight line, but it's colorful, connected, and full of discovery. And maybe that's the real beauty of it — that curiosity, not passion, has been guiding me all along. Hearing these words from Elizabeth Gilbert created a lightbulb moment—a real *"ah-ha"* kind of insight into why I've always bounced from one fulfilling career milestone to the next. And just like that, I realized: there's absolutely nothing wrong with me. I'm not broken—I'm just wired a little differently (Elizabeth Gilbert). https://www.youtube.com/watch?v=Z_PSUskgiZU

One thing I've always known about myself is that I *love* helping people. It's my thing. If someone needs a hand, I'm there—no hesitation. I even dubbed myself "The Helper" and proudly let everyone close to me know: *If you need me, just ask.* If I can show up, I will. If I can't, we'll still figure it out together like a team with snacks. But I'll never forget the moment that title— "The Helper"—got put to the test... when tragedy hit home. That's when helping stopped being just something I enjoyed and became something deeper, more personal.

I spent exactly six months in Job Corps, and honestly, it was just what I needed—even though my family had a whole lot to say about it. They did their best to talk me out of it, claiming it wasn't the right place for someone who had actually finished high school. But what they didn't get was that I wasn't just looking for a program—I was looking for *peace*. I was hurting, and I needed somewhere to figure myself out, to breathe, and to be far, *far* away from all the noise.

The truth is, no one ever really asked me what I wanted to do after high school—not my mom, not a teacher, not a counselor, *nobody*. The only person I know who *would've* asked, who would've actually cared and helped guide me, was Momo. She came from a whole line of educated folks. Her sisters up in Chicago owned and operated a barber school, her family-owned land. Like I mentioned before, she herself was a retired elementary school teacher. She understood what it meant to invest in your future—and if she'd still been around, I know she would've been in my corner, helping me figure out my next step instead of leaving me to figure it out on my own.

I eventually became a schoolteacher—go figure—even though teaching wasn't exactly at the top of my dream job list. I'd worked in the Department of Education for years, but I never imagined myself standing at the front of a classroom full-time. It wasn't even *my* idea, honestly. A colleague convinced me to apply for an accelerated teaching program, and that's what kicked off my unexpected journey into the world of education, teaching middle and high school students. And just like that, boom—I was a teacher.

Back in Job Corps, they offered all kinds of trades, and I went with what I thought was the most practical at the time—nursing assistant. I liked the structure, and my instructors were no-nonsense, firm, and definitely had high expectations. I'm pretty sure they had reputations to protect, especially when we got sent out to do our fieldwork. They did *not* want their names tied to any mess-ups out in the real world.

I actually picked up the basics pretty well and took to the hands-on work of a nursing assistant. But let me tell you what they *didn't* mention—how *real* it gets. Nobody warned us about the not-so-glamorous parts, like bathing patients or changing soiled bedding. That info came *after* graduation—surprise!

Still, I'll say this: it was a solid experience. I learned a lot, and I met some amazing people from all over the country—North, South, and everywhere in between. We kept in touch for a while, sharing stories and updates, but like most things in life, time passed and we slowly drifted. Still, I'll always look back on that chapter with a smile—and maybe a little side-eye at those "surprise" job duties.

The nightmare was finally starting to become a part of my past, and the way I escaped all the chaos it brought gave my soul a much-needed sigh of relief. I could slowly see the light creeping in—breaking through all the darkness that my younger self had long ago stopped believing would ever lift. No more put-downs. No more watching my mom carry sadness in her eyes. No more working in those fields under the blazing summer sun. No more constant reminders of what my life *could've* been if I had stayed. I was already moving through that tunnel—the one they say has no return—and I wasn't about to look back. The fear of my past, that darkness of my long night, was still close behind... and I knew if I looked back, it just might catch me.

Kind of like Lot's wife—you know, when she was told *not* to look back and did it anyway. Then, boom, she turned into a whole pillar of salt. Yeah... I wasn't about to go out like that. I *knew* what was waiting for me if I so much as took a quick peek. Nope. I kept my eyes straight ahead, locked on the prize I knew was waiting for me. One word: freedom. And I wasn't about to let a salty setback take me out.

Not every girl dreams of a fairy tale marriage, kids, white picket fences, and a happily ever after—some of us just dream of getting out of the nightmare. Those fairytales were for girls who grew up in way better conditions than me and my sister. Everything about our upbringing was mediocre, to say the least.

My dad, at best, was a decent father when my sister and I were still in our early childhood years. But that started to shift. Over time, things changed—*he* changed. And I guess, so did the way he showed up for us... or didn't.

Having more mouths to feed and a growing family to take care of seemed to pull my dad further away from us—the little girls he and my mom brought into this world. His attention shifted to everything *but* nurturing. There were no playful moments, no small talks, no quality time. It was all business, all seriousness, and a whole lot of stern commands. "I love you." Never heard it. Hugs? Not a chance. Affection just wasn't a thing, and for me and my siblings, *never* is exactly what we got. It makes me wonder if he just never got what he needed from his own parents—so the cycle just kept going.

3
"HE SEES YOU"
When God Chooses You

G rowing up as a little girl in church, I never really understood who God was—I just knew He sounded *terrifying*. I remember sitting through sermon after sermon where the main takeaway was "*Fear God... or else.*" So, I did. I feared Him in the *worst* way.

From what I could piece together, God was basically this angry, no-nonsense figure who was just waiting to catch you slipping. If you sinned, that was it—*straight to Hell*, no second chances, no do-overs, and definitely no "bless your heart" on the way down.

As I got older, I stayed scared. I wasn't a bad kid or anything, but I had my moments—mostly when I got sassy with my parents. And by sassy, I mean talking back *under my breath* because I wasn't trying to get smacked into next week. My dad especially had a short fuse, so breathing wrong could get you yelled at. And there I was, thinking every time I rolled my eyes or mumbled something slick, God was up there ready to push the smite button like, "*That's it, she's done.*" Let's just say my early theology was a mix of fire, brimstone, and trying not to die before bedtime.

When I was younger, I didn't really know much about God, church, or religion—except that every pastoral Sunday, I was *going* to church whether I liked it or not. No excuses, no negotiations. I'd go to Sunday school, sit through the Bible stories, nod like I understood... but let's be real, I had *no idea* who God actually was. All I knew was that Hell sounded *hot*, and I didn't want any part of it. I definitely didn't want to make God mad, especially over something small like talking back or sneaking an extra piece of chicken. I tried to be good, I really did—but when I messed up? Whew, I would go into full prayer mode. I'm talking dramatic begging like, "Lord, please don't kill me tonight. I promise I'll do better tomorrow." That whole phase of life was lowkey terrifying. But every time I woke up the next morning and realized I *hadn't* been smitten in my sleep, I was like, "Okay! He forgave me *again*. We're good."

Then, I hit adolescence—and let's just say, my prayers got longer. I was a little more bold (but still under my breath, 'cause I wasn't crazy), especially when my parents told me or my sister to do something they could *clearly* do themselves. Like, get them a glass of water, change the channel on the television, or get the mail out of the mailbox. I was like, *You in the kitchen already. Get your own water, or you're sitting right there in the room with the TV. Get up and change it yourself.* But no, because they had children, and we must obey our parents as they had full authority over us. Therefore, we had no other choice but to obey or else get our butts beaten. I just knew God was up there like, *"Keep it up... I'm watching."* But hey, I survived childhood *and* teenage years, so I guess grace was working overtime!

I also used to wonder if God was watching everything my parents were putting us through. I mean, they weren't handicapped or anything, but they sure were treating this parenting thing as if we were their personal assistants. Now, when Momo and Pawpaw needed help, that made *sense*—they were older, barely getting around, and actually needed us. But Mama and Daddy?

Two fully capable, able-bodied folks out here acting like they were on bed rest 24/7. Of course, I wasn't bold enough to say any of this out loud. I wasn't trying to get popped in the mouth *or* smote by God for being "disobedient." So, I did what any guilt-ridden, heaven-fearing teen would do—I obeyed. Reluctantly, with a heavy sigh and dramatic eye roll (done *internally*, of course), but I obeyed. I was basically just trying to make it through my teen years without ending up in Hell *or* grounded for life.

Now, me and my siblings look back and laugh—*hard*. But then we stop mid-laugh like, "Wait... did we do this to *our* kids too?" And the answer is, yep. Sure did. Guilty as charged. My kids—now full-grown—could probably start a support group called "Children of the Overdelegated."

All I can do now is hope and pray the cycle stops with them. When they have families of their own, they'll lead with love, patience, and a healthier view of God—one that doesn't make their kids think He's out here handing out lightning bolts every time they roll their eyes. Because the truth is, God loves them no matter what. It's the *sin* He can't stand—not the kid.

It wasn't all that long ago that I finally started to understand this revelation and really grow in the knowledge of who God *actually* is—not the scary, angry version I was introduced to as a kid, but the real, loving, patient God. I know now, without a doubt, that God chose *me*—I didn't choose Him. He loves me unconditionally, and there's absolutely nothing I can say or do to change His mind about that. Trust me, I've tried.

For the longest time, I thought I had to earn His love—like I was applying for a spiritual credit card. Baptism? I've been baptized so many times, I'm surprised I didn't grow gills. I kept thinking, "Maybe *this* time it'll stick." But nope—it wasn't about the water. It was about the lack of knowledge, and I had plenty of that.

Now, I didn't come to this revelation all on my own. I've got to give credit where it's due—first to the Holy Spirit, then Pastor A.R. Bernard, and Prophet Lovy Elias. When I heard Prophet Lovy's teaching, I sat there like, *wait... what?!* my *mind was blown.* I realized I didn't know *any* of the real TRUTH about God, and I was like, *"Whew, I've got some serious unlearning to do."* It was like discovering you've been watching the wrong season of a show your whole life. It felt as if I had gone all the way back to when I first learned about God. I was so far behind that by the time I finally caught up, I was already standing in front of Him—like, "Okay God, I *finally* get it!" And He would say, "Took you long enough—come on in."

Honestly, I believe it's a *tragedy* to go through life and never truly know who your Creator is. And I don't mean just *knowing of* Him—but *really* knowing Him. Not the version people *told* us about—but the actual loving Creator who isn't sitting around with a smite button. That, to me, is the real tragedy—spending your whole life scared of someone who's been loving you the whole time.

I used to feel like I was the black sheep of God's children—like the one He loved, but from a distance. I thought I was the kid that was just a little *too far gone* to be saved, delivered, or even considered redeemable. I figured God had His favorites... and then there was *me*, somewhere on the "We'll see what happens" list.

I can't tell you the exact day I realized God had chosen me—but I *can* tell you the day I heard His voice loud and clear. And let me just say this—*nobody*, and I mean *nobody*, can convince me He isn't real after that. You can debate theology all day long, but I know what I heard. Case closed.

My sister, Teresa, would tell me of things God had either spoken to her or shown her, and I recall feeling like I was not saved enough so He didn't care to speak to me or show me things as He had done with her. There was one time in particular when she shared something God had told her, and I swear, the feeling of rejection hit me like a brick. I couldn't help but ask her, *"Why doesn't He speak to me? What am I doing wrong?"* I was convinced it was a sign that I was headed straight to Hell with no pit stops. And honestly, at the time, I *wasn't* living right—I was wrapped up in a situation with a married man, so yeah... my spiritual résumé had some red flags. But in my mind, that just confirmed what I already feared: God had favorites, and clearly, I wasn't one of them.

I'd never had any experiences or encounters with God the way that my sister, who is a pastor, was experiencing. I wouldn't say I envied her, but I felt like I was being ignored by God, or maybe I wasn't saved enough to hear His voice. I know now that God can speak to anyone at any time that He chooses. My sister has always had this spiritual thing going on—like, ever since high school. Or at least that's when I *finally* started noticing it. She was always trying to keep me and my best friend (who somehow became *her* best friend too) on the straight and narrow, whether we asked for it or not. Teresa was the official voice of reason in our little trio. She was always in our ear, saying stuff like, "You shouldn't say that," or "You know that's not right." And we were like, *"Girl, can we just live?"* Naturally, we started calling her *Miss Church Lady* because she was always trying to do the right thing—and making sure we *attempted* to do it too. Like we had our own personal spiritual referee.

I remember the time—Lord have mercy—when my dad had made me so mad (which, let's be real, was basically a *daily* occurrence), I turned to my sister and my best friend and said, "I wish Daddy was dead."

Immediately, Teresa hit me with the spiritual panic: *"Oooh Linda, God is gonna get you for saying that! You can't say that!"* She looked like she was ready to back away from me in case a lightning bolt came through the ceiling. Now, in my defense, my best friend's dad had already passed, and in my teenage mind, she had the *good life*—no one yelling, no one slamming doors, no one calling her everything but a child of God. So yeah, I said what I felt in the moment.

Of course, about two seconds later, I got scared. I was like, *"Okay God, I didn't mean it like that, please don't smite me in my sleep."* After that, I tried to keep my mouth shut when it came to wishing anything drastic. But I'm not going to lie—the dislike was real, and it only got stronger the longer I lived under his roof. Every shout, every fuss, every "Go get me the remote" (that was right next to him) moment just added fuel to the fire.

Teresa never once said how she felt about our daddy's mean and surly demeanor, but I'm sure she wished he wasn't like that towards us. We were girls, and we needed him to teach us about life, boys, and making the right choices. Instead, we had a tyrant, and we tried staying out of his way at all costs. Thank God for giving me Teresa as a sister. I'm not saying that she was an angel or someone who did the right thing all the time because she wasn't. But she was someone whom God chose to make His presence known at an early age of life. All I knew was that God was to be feared, and I feared Him badly. I can recall a time when my sister and I were young, and we were talking about a dream we had. We both had the same dream about a woman who was at the end of the very long hallway of the house we lived in that was next to the doorway of our bedroom. She had long jet-black hair, almost as if it was a wig, and she grabbed us and held us down and made us say our prayers. I think back to that conversation and can say that God has been present in our lives and has chosen us as His children, even when we knew very little or nothing of Him as little girls. It wasn't until the sudden and tragic death of the man I was involved with that I heard God's voice—loud and clear.

I'm more than sure God has always been trying to talk to me, but I was out here expecting some big, dramatic Hollywood moment—like thunder crashing, skies opening, and His voice booming from a burning bush, *"LINDAAAA!"* Just like He did with Moses. But let's be real—God doesn't usually roll like that. His voice? Still. Small. Quiet. The kind you really have to *pause your chaos* to hear. And me? I was usually too busy doing everything *but* listening—probably arguing with someone or overthinking life.

I had this idea that God would just grab my attention when He was *good and ready*—like He'd send an angel with a clipboard or something. But nope. Let me just say for the record: I was *so, so wrong*—yet again—in my understanding of how He moves. It turns out, He's been there the whole time... just waiting for me to stop being loud enough to actually hear Him.

It was honestly the saddest moment of my life—I felt like everything had just fallen apart, and life didn't seem worth living anymore. But then... He spoke. And I *heard* Him. Not in some big dramatic way, but in that still, small voice—and somehow, it was the loudest, clearest thing I've ever heard. And you know what I did next? I listened. Really listened. And it turned out to be one of the most beautiful, unforgettable experiences of my life. That was the moment I knew—without a single doubt—that God was real. He heard me. He saw me. He *answered* me. Prayers, tears, questions... all of it.

Now, I know you're probably like, "Okay, sis, so *when* did this all happen?" I promise I'm getting there—just hang with me a little longer while we take a few more scenic detours down memory lane.

Remember when I told you I grew up in church? Well, let me be more specific—*dragged* to church. My mama *never* missed a 4th Sunday, like it was a standing appointment with Jesus Himself. And if she was going, you better believe we were going too. It didn't matter if you had a fever, a limp, or a broken spirit—if you could walk (or be carried), you were going to church.

Now, 4th Sunday wasn't just *any* Sunday. That's when the pastor showed up to deliver "The Word" in all its full, long-winded glory. Every other Sunday was just Sunday school and warm-up worship, but 4th Sunday, that was game day. And guess where I had to sit? Right in the choir stand. Not because I could sing—oh no, I was just *placed* there. And of *all* the chairs, mine was *directly* behind the pulpit. So, there I was, front and center… well, technically *back and slightly to the right*, but you get it—smack behind the pastor while he delivered a sermon that felt longer than a CVS receipt. And those sermons had me fighting for my life not to nod off. I was out here doing Olympic-level head bobs, trying not to drool on myself, while the whole church had a clear view of my spiritual struggle. Church trauma? Yeah, I've got it—choir stand edition.

Before I knew it, I had fallen fast asleep with my head face-down on my folded arms that rested on the small banner that was separating the pulpit from the choir stand. Just as I was getting *just right* to fall deeper into the abyss, someone nudged me and told me to wake up.

Mom had managed to look over from where she was sitting at the piano and noticed I had drifted off and wasn't paying attention to what the pastor was saying—which, to be honest, was happening more times than not. I had no clue what he was preaching about, but the old folks seemed completely *enthralled* by his every word. He kept them laughing from time to time, but I didn't get it. If it was even possible, I felt he could cause the dead to fall deeper in sleep, and Jesus wouldn't be able to wake them at resurrection. I used to look down from the choir stand and survey the congregation to see if there was anyone else out there sitting bored out of their minds as I was. I caught Momo a few times looking like she was struggling to keep those windows to the soul open. I would smile and say to myself, *I'm not the only one in here falling asleep from this long, drawn-out torturous event that takes place every 4th Sunday.* A lot of people my age and a few years older knew this but were afraid to talk about it openly because we dare not talk about the Reverend's sermons. I didn't mean to be rude or anything, but I just didn't get his teachings at all because they bored me. Besides, I told you I had already made up in my mind that God was going to eventually get tired of me asking Him to forgive me and just send me to Hell, and I knew that was the last place I wanted to end up. But what could I do at such a young age? So, I thought, and thought, and one day it dawned on me.

I said to Teresa, "I can't wait until I turn fourteen, so I can choose if I'm gonna go to church or not." I don't know what made me think that or even believe that Mama would go along with it. I knew that the devil had gotten into me some kinda bad. Who in the hell did I think I was to tell Mama, the woman who would pinch, slap, probably even drop kick you if she knew that I was not going to church on any given Sunday, if I didn't feel like it? I don't know what had gotten into Mama I guess the devil was trying to kill two birds with one stone that day I confronted Mama about my decision to excuse myself from going to church. I had finally turned fourteen, and it was a Sunday morning, AKA "Get up and get dressed for church" day. But that morning, I decided I was feeling bold. I looked at Mama and said, "I'm not going to church today."

Now, normally, I'd expect her to hit me with the classic *"You better go get yourself ready before I give you something to really stay home about."* But instead, she just gave me *the look*. You know the one—the "I'm about to snatch your soul" stare. I froze. I didn't *dare* say I hated church either. Not after my last near-death experience when I said I hated Daddy. I had learned my lesson on throwing the word *"hate"* around too casually. But surprisingly... she said nothing. And just like that, I stayed home. No fight. No belt. No holy oil. I figured Satan must've been on a winning streak that day because somehow, *he got into Mama* and made her let me tell *her* what I was going to do—and not the other way around. Wild times.

I didn't push my luck too often, but every now and then, I'd test the waters—just to see how many Sundays I could get away with skipping church without Mama threatening to whip me because I didn't want to hear a pastor who was so stale that he could put a dying man out of his misery and send him on to glory—-It was that boring. I used to sit there wondering if the goal was salvation or sedation. Either way, I was trying to avoid both. I used to get a kick out of the old folks—like my grandparents. They *really* loved going to church. Honestly, I could see why. They could relate to the sermon because it was being preached by someone not much older than they were. So why wouldn't they enjoy it?

Me, on the other hand? I couldn't relate *at all*. Plus, I just wanted to stay home and sleep in after being up half the night watching TV or running my mouth on the phone. Priorities, you know?

Outside of church on 4th Sundays and Sunday school, God was pretty much *nonexistent* in our home conversations. But my grandparents? They were the closest thing I had to knowing who God was. They were full of love, and I absolutely adored them—especially my grandmother.

I'm not exactly sure why I gravitated more toward Momo than Pawpaw, but I did. I loved them both like crazy, but Teresa definitely had more of a Pawpaw connection, while I was Momo's little shadow. Still, the love we had for both of them ran deep.

Isn't it funny how God works? When Teresa and I became moms, my second child ended up being born *on* Momo's birthday, and Teresa's son was born *a day before* Pawpaw's birthday. I mean, seriously—what are the odds of that? Like I said before, God sees you... and He definitely chose me. What exactly He chose me for? Yeah, I've been trying to crack that code for years. I used to ask God all the time, "What is my purpose here? Because surely You didn't put me on this earth to be somebody's emotional (or literal) punching bag." I asked so often, you'd think I would've gotten a direct memo by now. But nope—I'm still waiting on the divine download.

Eventually, I just chalked it up to this: whatever His plan is, it clearly ain't finished yet, because I'm still here. So, there's got to be something I'm meant to do—whether that's helping someone else or someone helping me.

Wouldn't it be amazing if prayer closets came with a secret button for believers? Like, just push it when you're stuck, and boom—you're face-to-face with God like, "Okay Lord, quick question..." and He gives you a clear, step-by-step guide. No cryptic parables, no waiting for a sign in a dream, just straight-up instruction. Now that would be a holy life hack!

But then again, that whole divine hotline idea would totally defeat the purpose of having faith, wouldn't it? **Hebrews 11:1 (NIV)** says, *"Now faith is confidence in what we hope for and assurance about what we do not see."* I mean, where's the growth if God's just popping up every time we hit a bump in the road like some heavenly GPS? *"Turn left at patience... rerouting due to Disobedience."* Nah, that's not how it works. As much as I'd love a step-by-step guide, I've learned that trusting Him through the process—*even when the process feels like a mess*—is where the real growth happens.

Let's be real, how would we ever develop character, strength, or even a testimony if we didn't trip over a few trenches, scrape our knees, and maybe cry in the car a few times? God already knows how this thing ends. Thankfully, He's got the answers to life's toughest hurdles—even the ones we pretend don't exist until they show up with a megaphone. So now, I *try* to trust Him more and panic less... emphasis on *try* and *less*. Most days I'm doing okay—other days, I'm two seconds from Googling, "How to wrestle control back from God without consequences." 😬

Proverbs 3:5–6 (NKJV) says it best:

5 Trust in the Lord with all your heart, And lean not on your own understanding;

6 In all your ways acknowledge Him, And He shall direct your paths.

Beautiful, right? But let's not skip over the keyword I wrote earlier: *try.* Because listen, I **do** trust God—like, for real. I trust Him fully... *spiritually.*

But my **flesh?** Oh, she still thinks she's the CEO of "Fix-It-All Incorporated."

My trust issues aren't with God—they're with people. But that *residue* from being let down, overlooked, or left hanging? Yeah, it sneaks into my faith walk. I've watched God come through for others—last-minute miracles, breakthroughs at 11:59 p.m.—and I celebrate like it's mine... but deep down I whisper, *"Would He do that for me though?"*

That's when I trip myself up. Not because God isn't able, but because my **stinking thinking** gets in the way. I want things so badly sometimes that it's hard to get too excited—because disappointment? Whew. She's been a frequent visitor. And let me tell you, hope is heavy when you've carried it before and it didn't turn out how you prayed.

So yeah... I've got trust issues. And no, that's not cute. The Bible doesn't exactly sugarcoat it either. **James 1:6–8 (NLT)** comes in swinging:

6 But when you ask him, be sure that your faith is in God alone. Do not waver, for a person with divided loyalty is as unsettled as a wave of the sea that is blown and tossed by the wind.

7 Such people should not expect to receive anything from the Lord.

8 Their loyalty is divided between God and the world, and they are unstable in everything they do.

Whew. Basically: God's like, "Don't come up here asking for stuff while flinching at your own prayer, sis." And honestly? Fair.

Why *should* God move if I'm over here being all double-minded and dramatic? But listen—I've been working on it. *Me and the Holy Spirit have been in therapy sessions, okay?* And He's doing a **work** in me. I'm not as indecisive as I used to be. I don't stand in the toothpaste aisle for 27 minutes anymore, and I no longer pace the kitchen like I'm auditioning for *Chopped* over whether to microwave leftovers or cook something "fresh." Growth, y'all.

Now, when that ol' "Double-Minded Debbie" tries to rise up—you know, the version of me that wants to believe God but also wants a backup plan *just in case*—I shut her down. How? I grab the Word. I remind myself what God told Abraham:

As it is written: "I have made you a father of many nations." He is our father in the sight of God, in whom he believed—the God, who gives life to the dead and calls into beings things that were not **(Romans 4:17 NIV).**

That part. If God could speak nations into Abraham before he even had a crib to put a baby in, surely He can handle my little situation too.

Listen, I got really tired of being tossed around like a sock in a spin cycle—my mind was all over the place, and it was *mentally exhausting*. I was one overthinking session away from a full system crash. My brain felt like a tornado on a caffeine binge. I finally had to shut it down when I realized I was out here faking faith like I deserved an Oscar. And guess what? God already knew. So, I figured, *why keep up the act?* I wasn't fooling Him, and honestly, I wasn't even fooling myself. Cue the honesty altar call.

4

"BROKEN HEARTS"

Why Them and Why Now, God?

It was January 1984, and Momo had gotten really sick—we knew the cancer had taken a turn for the worse. I remember Daddy taking me, Teresa, and his mom to the hospital to visit her that evening. When I walked into the room, Momo was just lying there, not moving, and her heavy breathing really shook me. It was hard to watch. It bothered me so much that I asked Mom if I could stay at the hospital with her that night, and she said yes.

Maybe she agreed because Daddy's mom was staying too, so it gave her a chance to go home, rest, and come back in the morning. I was actually glad she trusted me enough to stay. I felt she believed I could handle being there—watching Momo as she slowly slipped away.

I sat up the whole night, just staring at her. Watching her chest rise and fall with help from the oxygen machine, I just kept thinking about how much I loved her. I didn't want her to go. I wanted her to get better and come home with us after she left the hospital. I really believed we'd get that chance.

Everything I saw unfolding right before my eyes told me differently—that she would not be coming home with us. As I look back on that day, I'm positive I sensed this when I arrived at her room and why I was adamant about staying the night there with her, just to be in her presence one last time.

I couldn't take my eyes off of her. Occasionally, I would walk out into the hallway to stretch my legs, but I'd quickly return and sit and stare at the woman who was my first teacher. The woman who taught me to read at the age of five. The woman who sang in church with the keenest voice I had ever heard. The woman who would make mullein tea for me and Teresa when we would fall ill from a bad cold. The woman whom I wanted to live forever. My Momo was slipping away to a place I had only heard about in church. That place is Heaven.

I didn't want her to go—not now. We had already lost Pawpaw, he preceded her in death just a few weeks prior, in December. Why did she have to leave me and Teresa, too? I had really hoped that if she got better, she'd come stay at our house. I pictured it perfectly—Mama, Teresa, and I taking care of her, loving on her, doing everything we could to make her feel surrounded by warmth and comfort. Pawpaw was already gone, and I knew she'd be missing him something awful, so I figured we could fill that space with all the love we had.

Before Mama and Daddy left to go home that night, I overheard the adults talking in those low, serious voices—the kind that immediately confirm your worst fears. I heard someone say Momo might not make it through the night. That's when I asked Mom if I could stay. I didn't want her to be alone, and I didn't want to miss a second of being near her.

Now usually, I was the scaredy-cat of the family. I hated when someone passed away—*hated* it. I was the kid who believed all the ghost stories, especially since folks in our family had a habit of casually mentioning how someone's spirit would hang around after they died like it was just normal post-life behavior. So yeah, me asking to stay the night? That was big. But this was Momo. And nothing—not even ghost stories—was going to keep me from being by her side.

One time, me and Teresa nearly *sweated ourselves into the afterlife* because we were too scared to sleep with our faces uncovered after a relative died. We were convinced—like, 100% sure—that their ghost was going to show up in our room that night. So naturally, we pulled the covers over our heads like that thin blanket was some kind of ghost-repellent force field. When Mama came in to check on us, we were both drenched—*soaked* from head to toe like we'd been running laps in a sauna. Our faces were pale, our skin was wrinkled, and we looked a hot, sweaty mess. She looked at us like we'd lost our minds, yelled, *"Get them covers off your heads before y'all suffocate!"*

We took them off—for all of five minutes. As soon as she left the room, we were right back under that blanket like it was a holy shield. Because listen, Mama's yelling is scary, but It was still not scarier than the idea of a spirit floating at the foot of our beds. Plus, a ghost encounter, that could be forever.

The next morning, Momo looked even worse than when I first arrived to visit her. I got up and stood by her bedside, watching as she struggled to breathe—even with the machine helping her. I looked into her face; she'd open her eyes just for a moment, and I held her hand as she lay there, so still. For some reason, I decided to step out into the hallway to use the pay phone and call Mama, just to see what time she'd be coming back to the hospital. We had a short conversation—probably no more than three minutes—then I hung up and headed straight back to Momo's room.

As I walked down the hall, I saw my dad's mom standing there, like she was waiting for me to turn the corner. The look on her face said everything I didn't want to hear. I never took my eyes off her, and deep down, I already knew. When I got close enough, she just wrapped her arms around me and said, *"She's gone, Linda."*

Just like that... Momo had slipped away while I was gone for only a few minutes. I asked Ma—that's what we called my dad's mom—if I could go in and see her. I walked into the room, and the nurse was gently removing the tubes. I looked at Momo and just cried as I held her hand. Her hands were still warm, and I clung to that warmth like it was my last lifeline—because it was the last sign of life I had left of her. I wanted her to open her eyes and look at me, just once more. I wanted her back. But I knew that was a request only God could answer—and sometimes, His answer is no. Still, I believe she knew I was there. I believe she felt me beside her as she gently slipped into everlasting life with God.

Then I realized, both my Momo and Pawpaw were gone. They couldn't be apart from each other here on earth, and it turns out, they wouldn't be apart in Heaven either. From then on, my mom has never enjoyed Christmas and New Year's because the people who raised her were no more on this side, and she felt she was alone in this world. I felt her pain. I was fourteen years old, and this was the only time I had ever lost anyone so close and dear to my heart—until that dreadful day in May 2011.

5
RELATIONSHIP #1: Ryan
What Have I Gotten Myself Into?

I didn't know *a thing* when it came to boys. I mean, absolutely *nothing*. Telling the good ones from the bad ones? Yeah... that skill was *not* in my toolbox. I went out into the world clueless, like a bat flying blind in broad daylight, just hoping for the best. Spoiler alert: the best didn't always show up. And don't forget—no one prepared me! The *one* person who should've sat me and Teresa down and given us the real deal, the do's and don'ts of dealing with the opposite sex, was too busy... being unbothered. My dad never made the time to teach us anything useful in that department. Not a warning, a heads-up, or even a "watch out for that one, he looks shifty." Nope. We were just out here raw-dogging life and winging it.

Besides, he probably didn't even *have* the communication skills to teach us anything useful. Add that to the fact that he was too busy doing his own thing, and his version of *parenting* was just flat-out forbidding me and Teresa from having a boyfriend, going on dates, or even going to the movies with one. That was his whole strategy—just say "no" and keep it moving. He was strict to the point of suffocating. Honestly, it made me dislike him *a lot*.

Meanwhile, I was at the age where boys were starting to notice me, and I was starting to kind of notice them back. But who was I supposed to talk to about it? I had no one. So, I did what many of us do—I figured I'd just *learn as I go.*

Now, is experience really the best teacher? When it comes to relationships? I'm going to go ahead and say, *Absolutely not.* Because when you're informed ahead of time, you might actually avoid some of those dead-end situations that come with heartbreak, confusion, and wasted time. Experience just has you out here kissing frog after frog, hoping *maybe* this one won't croak when he opens his mouth.

My dad will never truly know how much I needed him to *be* my dad—not just the man who helped bring me into the world, but a *real* father, present and connected to his daughters. He had the power to save us from so much pain, confusion, and deception, but he didn't.

The thirteen-year-old girl in me still wants him to know that she resents him for the horrible way he treated her and her siblings. The twenty-year-old me wants him to understand that he left behind a deep scar of neglect, the kind that only God Himself can heal. And the fifty-three-year-old woman I am today, she wants to tell him straight-up: he never should've been a parent. But how do you say that to a seventy-eight-year-old man who probably doesn't even remember, or worse—*doesn't care to* remember all the damaging things he said and did?

How do you look at him and say, "Hey, remember that one decent, kind young man who actually wanted to marry your daughter? Yeah, well... he never got the chance because *you* ran her away from home, and she ended up in an abusive relationship with nowhere to go and no real place to call home—all because you pushed her out instead of pulling her in."

And how do you say all that without feeling sorry for this now-fragile man, who thought fatherhood was just about keeping the lights on and food on the table? So instead, I did what I saw my mom do. I mimicked her survival. I stayed. I took the abuse, and I suffered in silence.

When I entered Job Corps, I had *no clue* what was about to happen—or how it would set my life on a path that only God Himself could help me navigate. I adjusted to the facility pretty quickly and actually started to like the place, even though, just like my grandma and mom said, most of the students there were high school dropouts. They *loved* reminding me of that, by the way. During my first week, I had to take an academic assessment to see where I ranked. I already knew I'd score in a high percentile—*I may have been young and confused, but I wasn't dumb*—and sure enough, I tested out of academic classes and got placed straight into the nursing assistant trade. I actually enjoyed the course and found myself genuinely interested in what the beginner side of nursing looked like. My plan was simple: finish the program, maybe become a nurse, and do something with myself.

That was the plan... **Until I met a boy.** And yep, you already know—*that* was the plot twist. He was from New York, and I loved his accent. There was nothing particularly cute about him, but something about him caught my attention. I didn't realize until later in life that it was his charisma—the same quality that kept getting me into trouble with men. He never even noticed me until one day when he walked past my classroom window and I gasped, loud enough to catch the attention of a classmate who just so happened to live in the same dorm as this New Yorker. As soon as he heard my reaction, I knew my secret crush wasn't a secret anymore.

He turned to me and said, "You like Brooklyn?" That was the boy's campus nickname. I blurted out a shy, "No, I just like the way he talks." Before the day was even over, word had gotten back to Brooklyn that someone had a crush on him. Next thing I knew, I was his girlfriend—all because I loved that New York swagger and the way he talked, just like the rappers I saw on TV. He had the colored high-top fade, could dance like nobody's business, and moved just like Kid-N-Play. He was smooth. I had always dreamed of going to New York or L.A., and here he was, possibly my ticket out.

It didn't take long before I was head over heels. Other boys would ask, "What do you see in him? You're a pretty girl." But for me, it wasn't about looks—it was his charm. I won't talk about his lack of... conventional attractiveness, but let's just say beauty is in the eye of the beholder. Because I chose to be with him, other boys who were interested in me didn't take it well. One boy and his cousins would say slick stuff to get Brooklyn riled up, and yes—fights happened. I hated walking into the cafeteria with him because it felt like everyone was watching us, watching *me* for choosing him and *him* for being chosen. But despite all that, I stuck beside him. Outside of the drama, he was fun to be around—cool, chill, and he eventually opened up.

The thing about Job Corps is, you don't really get to know who you're dating. Between the rules and structure, you only see the surface-level version of people, which can be very misleading. It wasn't until I visited New York that I got a real look at who he really was.

During my six months at Job Corps, I completed the nursing assistant program and earned my certificate. Afterward, I decided to head back home, get a job, save money, and finally leave Mississippi for good. Brooklyn stayed behind at Job Corps, but we kept our relationship going long-distance. I landed a job not long after I got back and stayed focused on my goal. I was determined—nothing was going to stop me but death. I already had my New York connection, so housing wasn't an issue. All I had to do was save, buy a ticket, and go.

I started working at a nursing home, which later led to a hospital job I was *very* happy to accept. I did both jobs for a while until I left the nursing home—the smell alone could send you running, and the heavy lifting nearly broke my back. I was so relieved when I got the hospital job, where the patients were more independent and less, well... smelly. No more changing bedpans and lifting grown people solo. That hospital job gave me time to figure out if nursing was really what I wanted. I considered becoming an LPN, especially since I enjoyed talking with the patients. It reminded me of my grandparents, and in a way, it felt like I was honoring Momo and Pawpaw. Older folks are a lot like kids—they say what they mean, offer solid advice, and you always learn something.

Eventually, it was time to go. I had saved up enough money for my one-way ticket and wasn't looking back. I didn't tell anyone, not even Teresa. Everyone thought I was just going to visit my boyfriend for a few days. I knew better. I had no plans to come back. I was done with Mississippi, done with living under my parents' roof, and definitely done seeing my dad's face every day.

I hopped on that Greyhound bus and rode for what felt like forever—nearly three days. I was nervous and wondering if New York would look like the movies. Spoiler: it did. As soon as I got off the bus at Port Authority, it was *exactly* what I imagined—homeless folks, cardboard beds, the works. I didn't see Ryan (Brooklyn) anywhere and started to panic a little. I found a pay phone and called his house. Someone told me, "He's on his way."

Whew. That was a relief, but I was still shocked he wasn't there waiting. This was a whole new city, and I didn't know a soul. I stood in one spot scanning every face until finally, about 20 minutes later, I spotted him. My nerves calmed instantly. I told him New York was *exactly* like what I'd seen on TV. He laughed.

We hopped on the subway from Penn Station to Coney Island, Brooklyn. On my first subway ride, I was wide-eyed the whole way. The excitement of being in a new place, with my boyfriend, starting a whole new chapter—it was a lot, but it was the kind of "a lot" I had prayed for.

Coney Island was freezing, but beautiful. The view of the Atlantic Ocean across from the apartment complex (aka the projects) was stunning. Everything felt fresh and exciting. The boardwalk, especially in the summer, was alive. I loved visiting the amusement park, hanging out with Ryan's sister, and just soaking in my new world. My first real sightseeing adventure was Rockefeller Center, and let me tell you—it was just like the movies. The lights, the cabs, the chaos... all of it. I had officially arrived.

I figured once I got to New York, Ryan would take me around the neighborhood, show me the sights, maybe do something fun and exciting. Yeah... that never happened. And honestly, that should've been the first red flag waving in my face. After a few weeks of being there and the initial excitement wore off, I realized we never went anywhere together—like, *ever*. I was always stuck in the house, and he barely left unless it was the weekend.

Looking back, his lack of interest in spending time with me or taking me out should've been a major "something ain't right" alert. I mean, he was all over me at Job Corps, so I expected that same energy out in the real world. But nope. Reality hit hard, and it was clear—this wasn't campus life anymore, and I was definitely no longer in Mississippi... but I sure felt confined like I still was.

I was never the adventurous or tourist type, so visiting places like the Statue of Liberty and all those things people do when they come to NYC never interested me one bit. I was perfectly content just being in a new place. But after a while, it did start to baffle me that I hadn't been shown *anything*—not even the basics. It finally hit me that something about this whole setup was off.

It was December 1989 when I arrived in the city I thought I'd eventually call home. Not long after that, I found out I was expecting. I had always known I wanted to have a child—just not so soon and definitely not at twenty. I remember calling home and breaking the news to my mom. Her voice was stern and straight to the point when she said, "You better not be." And all I could say was, "Ma, I don't live there anymore."

I remember thinking, *How can she say that to me now?* Like, I didn't get any talks growing up about this stuff, and suddenly it's a problem? She hit me with the whole "I didn't raise you to be shacking up" line, and in my head, I was like, *Well, I'm not coming back home anyway, so what difference does it make if I'm pregnant?*

She wasn't wrong about the shacking-up part—and I can admit that now—but why couldn't conversations like this have happened *before* I moved away? The one thing I did see my mom and dad do right, at least biblically, was getting married before starting a family. That was the one positive example I had growing up. And yet, here I was—the first of my siblings (at the time) to break that mold and not follow God's instructions on that part.

Teresa and my brothers did it the way God intended—married first, then started their families. They followed the blueprint. Me? Not so much. It wasn't like I set out to go against God's will on purpose. I wasn't trying to rebel. I just didn't fully understand what being "grown" actually meant. When you're young and thinking you've got it all figured out, life has a funny way of showing you otherwise.

So yeah, I got pregnant before marriage. That's a choice I have to live with. But let me be clear—abortion was never on the table for me. I knew that much. I accepted the responsibility and kept pushing forward, even if I didn't do things in the "right" order. **Genesis 2:24 (NIV)**,

"That is why a man leaves his father and mother and is united to his wife, and they become one flesh."

Not even a full year into living in New York with my boyfriend, and the pregnancy still fresh, the physical abuse started. I can't even remember the exact moment it began or what triggered it—but suddenly, I was in this dark, heavy space that felt nothing like the new life I thought I was starting. It usually started with arguments. Then, it quickly escalated to him putting his hands on me.

When it got to be too much—when I couldn't take another moment of it—I picked up the phone and called home. I told Mom I was coming back. That call felt surreal. I had sworn I'd never return to Mississippi to stay—maybe visit, sure, but live there again? Never. And now, the very place I was so desperate to escape had become the only place that felt safe. I remember thinking, *God...what did I get myself into?*

There was a lot of pleading and begging for me not to leave, but I had made up my mind—I was out, pregnant or not. I'd already seen this kind of toxic environment growing up, and I didn't want to live through it again, let alone raise a child in it. But at the same time, I kept thinking, *my baby should have a father in his or her life.* Still, that wasn't enough to keep me there. So, just like that, I packed up and left New York, about five or six months pregnant, and headed back to Mississippi.

I had accepted that my child would be born in the South and that I'd be a single mom. I never really talked to either of my parents about why I was back—I definitely wasn't on speaking terms with my dad. If things had been better between us, maybe I would've opened up. But I already knew how that conversation would've gone. They probably would've tried to talk me out of going back to New York, especially after all the "I'm sorry" phone calls I kept getting. Honestly, I wasn't ready to hear any of it.

I returned after a month and a half later in hopes that he was genuinely remorseful and it wouldn't happen again. I was deceived; not only did it continue, but it intensified. I knew I couldn't keep running home whenever I had enough because it would be too costly. So, I stayed.

By the time my son turned two, I really started thinking more seriously about a career. Having this little person depending on me lit a fire under me. I knew if I kept putting off going back to school or furthering my education, I'd risk getting too comfortable—stuck in the same place, settling for something mediocre. And that just wasn't the future I wanted for either of us so, I decided to move back home and enroll in college in Meridian. I also wanted Ryan to be involved in our child's life, so I encouraged him to apply too—and he actually did. At the time, it felt like a good move. I mean, let's be real—success without putting in any real effort doesn't feel like success at all. It leaves you stuck, with no real growth.

Now, you might be wondering, *Was I still dealing with abuse during all this?* The short answer? Yes. The thing with abusers is—they'll keep going until the person they're hurting finally makes a choice to walk away. It takes an average of **7 attempts** for a survivor to leave an abusive relationship for good (*DomesticShelters.org*). But if you grew up like I did—seeing dysfunction and thinking it was just a normal part of keeping a family together—you don't leave. You stay. You keep trying. Because deep down, you just want your family to work, no matter how broken it is.

I never saw my dad put his hands on my mom, but they definitely argued—a lot. I never really understood why she stayed, but looking back, I guess I stayed for the same reason. I had a child with this guy. Therefore, in my mind, that meant I was supposed to try and make it work. You either hope he'll change, or you keep going down the same toxic path until something finally breaks—whether that's you, him, or the whole relationship.

The abuse didn't stop. I just got used to it, as wild as that sounds. I settled into the dysfunction. Eventually, I started fighting back. Not because I thought it would fix anything—but because I had reached my limit and was tired of him thinking he was in control of me. When I started fighting back, it was like he had this moment of shock—like, *Oh no she didn't just lay hands on me!* You could almost see it on his face, like he was thinking, *Who does she think she is, standing up for herself?* It was as if he had lost his superpower and got weaker with every fight we had.

All three of us were back in Mississippi now. Since I didn't have a car to get to and from class, I decided to stay on campus. My mom stepped in to take care of my son. Honestly, I knew he was in good hands with her and my siblings around. I'd head home on the weekends to spend time with him and catch up with the family.

Things were going well between Ryan and me; he lived across the street at the co-ed dormitory, and I lived on the other side where the campus was in the girl's dormitory. I quickly acclimated to my schedule and became acquainted with a few girls in the dorm. I realized Ryan and I needed to be apart; we were always around each other every waking day in New York, but here, there was a chance for me to experience being around other people besides him and his family. Things were finally looking better for me, and I didn't have to wonder if this would be a day of arguing and fighting. I had peace, and I was moving on.

Soon things between Ryan and me started to shift. He was building a new life somewhere else and growing more distant by the day. I noticed it—and honestly, I was kind of okay with the space. But at the same time, I still loved him. A part of me probably hoped we'd eventually find our way back to each other. Still, as I watched him getting more caught up in his own world, I figured it was only a matter of time before he moved on and got involved with someone else—child or no child. And if I'm being real, I didn't know how I'd feel about that. Like I said, I still had love for him.

But eventually, that started to change. The distance between us created space for me to start thinking about dating again. Not that I was actively looking—but the idea crossed my mind. At first, it felt like a stretch. I mean, I was a young mom with a baby. Who would want to date someone who already came with a family? As it turns out... I was about to find out.

One random evening as I'm standing outside my dorm with my dormmates this guy pulls up. I kind of noticed him but thought I couldn't possibly be his type. He was nice looking. Back then my self-esteem was shot due to the abuse. I was watching this specimen of a man walk towards my direction, and he stepped to me as if I was the only one standing there and began talking to me. Just like that, I met a new guy and began dating.

Denzel was in the Navy and was stationed in Meridian. He was kind, a perfect gentleman, and I quickly fell for him. Ryan was now a thing of the past, and I loved every waking day of knowing this reality. I took hold of it and held on as if my very life depended on it. I was free. Until...

One beautiful evening, I was just chilling in my room on campus when someone called from the front desk saying I had a visitor. Naturally, I assumed it was Denzel—but nope. To my surprise, it was Ryan. I remember thinking, *What in the world would bring him across the street?* Especially since we weren't exactly on speaking terms. I figured he must've been feeling froggy and decided to hop across campus to try and act like we were still a thing. Maybe he wanted to see if he still had some kind of control over me. I don't remember all the details that led to the argument, but I clearly remember saying something like, "We're not together anymore. I'm done with you." That must've hit a nerve, because next thing I know, he pushed me—hard. I hit the ground, hurt my wrist, and he just casually walked away like nothing happened.

With tears in my eyes, I stood up and dusted myself off, holding my wrist, and made my way back to my room. One of the girls saw I was upset and asked what happened. I tried to brush it off like I was fine, but she wasn't buying it. She told me, "You need to report his ass." And before I could even think about it, she went straight to the RA, who called the cops. A report was filed, and Ryan was arrested.

Part of me felt bad—he was so far from home, and now this? But at the same time, he needed to learn that he couldn't just bring that same mess he pulled in New York down here and think there'd be no consequences. He wasn't allowed to come near me for the rest of my time on campus, and for that—I was truly thankful.

So, after Ryan's little run-in with the law and things settled back into college life, he finally realized he couldn't pull the same mess down here that he used to get away with in New York. Suddenly, he decided he wanted to keep our son on campus with him for the weekend. Now, as a young mom, I never kept my son away from his dad—I wasn't that kind of parent. Plus, honestly, it was about time he spent some quality dad time anyway. So, I agreed. That Friday, just like we planned, my mom came to pick me up so I could go home for the weekend, and she brought my son with her. I handed him over to his dad to spend the weekend together, and the plan was for my mom and sister to bring him back when they dropped me off at campus on Sunday. Easy enough, right? What could possibly go wrong? (Spoiler alert: something always does.)

I never told anyone in my family that I was being abused—probably out of shame and definitely because I didn't want to find out what would happen if my dad ever got wind of it. But my mom? She got a front-row seat to the kind of anger the father of my child was capable of.

It was the end of the weekend, time for me to head back to campus, and father-son bonding time was officially over. I called Ryan to let him know we were on the way to pick up my son, but of course, he decided he "wasn't ready" for the visit to be over and said he wanted more time. Never mind that it was already getting late and my mom had to drive back home. None of that mattered to him. So, while we sat there in the car waiting for him to gather our son's things, he decided to show out. He finally came out with our son and started trying to pick a fight with me. When I refused to take the bait, he grabbed all of my son's clothes and tossed them out onto the ground—right there in the middle of campus—then turned around and walked back inside like he had just done something noble. It was embarrassing. But more than that, it was the moment my mom saw for herself the kind of person I'd been dealing with.

My mom could not believe what she had just witnessed. That made her so angry, and she never liked his ass after that episode, but I still did not disclose the abuse I endured when I was in New York, nor the recent one that got him arrested here. I'm sure that parents know when things aren't right with a child, and I want to believe that both my Mama and Daddy knew of my abuse at some point because they had expressed their lack of approval towards Ryan. To this day, I wonder how they could have known or found out. I guess its parent intuition.

My relationship with Denzel was starting to develop into something serious, and I wanted to see where it would take us. He included me in a lot of what he did—we went out, he visited often, and I spent time with him on base whenever I could.

When school let out for the summer, I headed back to my parents' house. I didn't really think through what it would be like being back under their roof, especially since my relationship with my dad was still strained. But I tried to stay humble, keep my head clear of childhood trauma, and did my best to avoid being in his presence.

I was not happy but content because I needed to keep my son safe and have a place to stay and be at peace. That soon ended when my dad and I got into a heated argument when I heard him curse at my dear precious baby. This was where I drew the line. As a child, I had no other choice but to take his put-downs and cursing me and siblings out, calling us motherfuckers, bastards, and saying, "You ain't gonna be shit." But I wasn't having it, and the line was drawn in the sand that evening when it came to my child, my baby, my two-year-old.

It got to the point where he put his hands on me. Before I knew it, I was out the door with my child in my arms, calling Denzel to come get me. I couldn't believe that was happening—again. It felt like déjà vu, and I was tired. Tired of these so-called men who thought love looked like control, like dominance, like putting their hands on me when I didn't fall in line. Why did they think I needed to be controlled? Why did my refusal to submit mean I had to be punished? I wasn't a child. I didn't need to be disciplined. And I certainly didn't deserve to be broken by two people who clearly didn't understand the damage they were doing—or worse, didn't care.

Denzel arrived, confused about everything that had just happened. As we're walking out the door of my parents' home, Daddy decided to turn into an even bigger asshole. He grabbed his pistol and fired it into the ceiling—like that was supposed to prove some kind of point.

From living in New York, I knew that when a man pulled a gun, he usually planned to use it—not just wave it around to scare somebody. I also knew he didn't approve of Denzel either. Honestly, I didn't give a damn. He didn't want either of his daughters to be with anyone for that matter. Well, he missed his chance to be a real father a long time ago—missed the chance to teach me or Teresa anything about boys or men. That train had already left the station and wasn't coming back. All of that was completely unnecessary. What point was he trying to make?

If that bullet had come back down and hit me, I probably would've welcomed it. It would've felt like a release from the hell I was already living in—and the hell I was about to walk into again for years to come. I asked myself, *God... what did I do to deserve this?*

Denzel got a room at a hotel for us to stay the night. I told him everything that had happened and that I couldn't go back—not to that house, not to that environment. At that point, I was technically homeless. I had nowhere to go and was left choosing between the lesser of two evils, which honestly felt exactly the same. You could say I was stuck between a rock and a hard place.

Denzel started throwing out all kinds of solutions, trying to figure out what we could do—but nothing made sense to me at the time. My mind was all over the place. I needed to calm down and think clearly, but I couldn't. The only decision I could come up with was to pack up my things and go back to New York.

It felt like everything I was starting to build for myself just wasn't meant to be. Like maybe I wasn't meant for peace, or love, or stability—that I was just destined to live a life of constant struggle and despair. I didn't want to go back. I wanted to stay. I wanted to finish college. I wanted to be with the man I had fallen for.

Denzel didn't realize just how much he meant to me—or how much he had changed the way I saw relationships. I wanted more with him, and I truly believed we were headed somewhere good. He had a steady career in the military, and I was starting one in the medical field. We were on the right track, and I wanted to see where it could go.

I ended up back in New York with my son. Things weren't exactly great, but they were not terrible either—just kind of existing, given the situation I was in. But Denzel? He was constantly on my mind. After being back for a while, I decided to call and check in to see how he's doing.

I ended up telling him something he probably didn't want to hear—and honestly, I wasn't even sure if I *should* tell him. But I did. His response? "If you are, I'm coming to get you." We exchanged a few more words, and then he said something that hit differently—something that made me question where we really stood. My heart sank. We ended the call. I didn't call him again, and just like that, he was out of my life but not out of my mind or my heart. I sensed, in my heart, that I hurt him when I decided to return to New York. I found out just how much his heart was wounded when we found each other again twenty-eight years later.

At that point, I was doing my best to make the most out of a bad situation—in a place I didn't want to be, carrying a child I wasn't exactly prepared for. Yes, I was pregnant. Again. I was not even sure how far along, or if it happened before I left for New York or after I came back, trying—*hoping*—to get to a place of calm with the father of my son.

We tried to start over. Tried to hit the reset button and pray it actually worked this time. Apologies were said, sure—but they weren't sincere. They were just words, spoken to quiet me down. To keep me there. And for a moment, they worked.

But then reality crept back in. The arguments started. Then the fighting. And I found myself staring down the same storm I had barely made it out of the first time. This time I had another child on the way. I thought, *What am I going to do with a second baby in a toxic environment? How did I end up here—again?*

Still, something in me held on. I stayed. I didn't run home this time. I braced myself. I endured. Just like I did before. Only this time, I kept whispering to myself: *Focus on the positive. Try to believe it'll get better.* But even that becomes hard when survival starts to look like silence.

I gave birth on May 17, 1993. It was a baby boy. At that point, I had suppressed the thoughts of who the father could possibly be, especially when my mind was on all that was happening in my very toxic relationship with Ryan. I dealt with it because it was my fault for coming back this time, but I had no place to go but here.

I figured that Ryan had realized he no longer had a hold on me like before, and there was someone out there who appreciated me. With that reality, I thought maybe he would be different...treat me better. I was wrong. There was no change.

I was numb at that point—void of any real hope for change in my life. I was in survival mode. With two young bodies to care for, and no real hope of having the support I so desperately needed.

I was in mommy mode, thinking only of creating a solid foundation and environment for them to grow. My mind was in a state of shock, disbelief, uncertainty, and fear. Fear of the unknown. Fear of failing. Fear gripped my mind constantly. *How does one function without losing it?* I wondered.

I was on autopilot—numb to the abuse, whether it was mental or physical. My children were my only reality, the only thing that kept me sane and gave me a purpose: to live, to provide, and to create a future for them that looked nothing like my past.

I eventually took a summer trip back to Mississippi with the boys. I loved visiting in the summer—it gave the kids a chance to play outside and actually enjoy being outdoors. My baby was about six months old and growing so fast. I'd often stare at him, searching his little face for features he might share with my oldest—but I didn't see any.

The thought that he might be Denzel's child kept me in this uneasy, anxious state. *What do I do? What do I say? Do I tell Ryan that the baby might not be his? Do I tell Denzel?* God, the weight of it all had me in a chokehold— like a boa constrictor tightening around me.

That grip would eventually loosen... but not because the situation got better. No, it faded because a much bigger, more dangerous monster was waiting for me—one more powerful than confusion. That monster was jealousy, control, and anger—all rolled into one—and it dragged me into a whole new kind of chaos. How could one person carry so much anger and evil inside? Why would someone want to exert power over another person when it was clear that it was causing them pain? Why would you want someone to feel hurt just because *you're* broken? Wouldn't you want to escape that darkness and let someone shine a little light into those heavy, hidden places in your heart?

I guess Ryan was too broken—and, truthfully, so was I. So instead of healing, he chose pain. And he wanted me to feel every bit of his too.

During our visit back home, Teresa's nonstop taunts about my baby not being Ryan's were too much for my already fragile mental state. She was relentless—like a mosquito that just wouldn't quit. I wanted to slap her so hard that she'd see all the way back to the day she was conceived. But that was

Teresa for you—always in somebody's business that didn't involve her. You'd think she'd have learned to mind her own after the beating Daddy gave her for exposing his cheating ways, but nope—some lessons just didn't stick.

And truth be told, she was probably right, no matter how hard I tried to suppress the thought. Her teasing was like a broken record I couldn't turn off. By that point, Denzel was in my past—probably off somewhere thriving in the Navy, living his best life. And even if I *wanted* to reach out, I wouldn't even know where to start looking.

Just recently, while visiting home during COVID-19 in October 2022, I found myself randomly searching for Denzel on social media. Those thoughts that I had suppressed so many years ago came rushing back. For some strange reason, I felt led to look him up again. It had been twenty-eight years since we'd seen or heard from each other. My brother happened to be visiting too, and I told him how Teresa used to tease me about my son possibly being Denzel's. He said he remembered hearing her say it so much that even *he* started to wonder. He admitted he had noticed some things about the baby back then that made him think, *Maybe Teresa was on to something after all.*

Now back to that summer.

When I decided to head back to New York, I knew I had to get serious about my life. I needed to focus on building a career—something that would give me independence and stability. I applied for public assistance. Honestly, I felt ashamed. I was the first in my family to ever need it, and I knew from day one that it was just a steppingstone, not a permanent solution.

But I'll give credit where it's due—public assistance opened up opportunities I didn't even know existed. They had programs that allowed single moms to attend college while their kids were enrolled in on-campus elementary school. It felt like the perfect setup, the chance to finally finish what I'd started back when I was in college in Mississippi. And yep, I encouraged Ryan to take advantage too—again.

This time, I was determined. Nothing was going to stop me from getting that degree. I was still torn about what to major in, though. Nursing no longer sparked my interest, but I was still drawn to science and fascinated by the human body. So, I went for an associate's degree in Science. When I graduated, I felt proud—really proud—but I also knew deep down that I wasn't done yet. I wanted more.

On the other hand, Ryan didn't finish college—just like he hadn't finished much of anything else when it came to school. You can't force someone to want better for themselves, especially when it comes to education. No matter how much you push, they have to want it for themselves. I should've seen the signs, but I was too wrapped up in life—raising my boys, juggling everything else—to notice the pattern playing out right in front of me.

Ryan had dropped out of high school, got his GED, didn't finish college in Mississippi, and now he was doing the same thing in New York. He had no drive, no motivation—just stuck in the same cycle he was used to. But I wasn't about to let that cycle continue with my kids. I made it my mission to raise my boys differently, to show them there was more to life than just surviving. I refused to let them become another sad statistic.

The abuse was still happening, and I was beyond tired of trying to make something work that was clearly draining the life out of me. I didn't know what to do anymore. I remember having a conversation with Ryan's sister one day, and she told me straight up that she knew what her brother was doing. She said he would intentionally start arguments with me anytime I mentioned needing a little *me time*—which wasn't often—whether it was to hang out with friends or even with *her*.

Hearing that from her actually brought me a weird kind of relief. I really liked her—she was kind to me, and it meant a lot that she didn't agree with how her brother treated me. After that conversation, she looked at me and said, "Get up, get dressed, and leave. Get on the bus and ride it to the last stop. Just get out of the apartment and make him wonder where you are."

That's exactly what I did. And just like she predicted, he immediately wanted to know where I'd been. She also told me that one time, when I was about to go somewhere—either with her or someone else—Ryan turned to her and said, "Watch me go make her change her mind." And he did. He had done that same thing so many times, on purpose, just to keep me from going anywhere. Control—it was his favorite trick.

How could someone who had absolutely nothing going for themselves be so abusive and controlling? I couldn't wrap my head around that kind of behavior. People would say, "I don't know where he got that from," but I never bought into that. He learned it from *somewhere*.

To me, he was weak—and the only way he knew how to feel powerful was by exerting control over me. I was in New York, with no family, no real support system. I was completely alone, and he knew it. He used that truth to his full advantage.

At one point, I had the chance to move out of the apartment I shared with Ryan and his family. A friend who lived in the same building offered me a place to stay, and I took it. It was a much-needed, although brief, separation. For the first time in a long while, I got to experience what life felt like without being in Ryan's presence every single day. I'm sure he needed the space just as much as I did.

But eventually, I found myself back downstairs. Just like that, life picked up where it left off. I had assumed, or maybe *hoped*, that this time apart would motivate Ryan to get serious about our situation. I thought maybe he'd want to move out of his mom's place and finally get an apartment for just us and the kids. But I was wrong. It became clear that he had no intention of doing any of that. He was never motivated to take a single step toward what a real man would've done for his family.

He was perfectly content living at his mom's place—with his sister, her family, me, and the boys all under one roof. As for work, jobs were few and far between for him. He bounced between seasonal gigs and random construction jobs that could last a day, a few weeks, or if we were lucky, a couple of months.

Then out of nowhere, he hit me with the news—he was moving to Atlanta. I was like, *Wait… without us?* And just like that, he said yes, as if it was no big deal. He didn't care that he was leaving me to raise the kids on my own. No conversation, no plan—nothing. He just left. Poof. Gone.

A few months later, he showed back up—no explanation, no reason, just back like he'd never left. I could only assume that the friend who invited him down to Atlanta finally saw what I had been dealing with for years. Maybe he saw the liar, the deadbeat, the unreliable and incompetent man I came to know all too well once we started living together.

Ryan had always been a great pretender—a smooth talker, a deceiver. But at some point, you've got to get tired. Tired of wearing the mask. Tired of putting on a show. Pretending to be someone you're not has to be exhausting. And honestly? Probably a little depressing too.

I know you're probably thinking, *Girl, what is it going to take for you to get out of this mess? Haven't you had enough? The writing is on the wall—He. Does. Not. Want. You.* And trust me, I hear you.

But remember my childhood? Remember how I grew up watching everything my mom did and thinking that's just what you're *supposed* to do? Well, that's why I stayed. I thought I was doing what was expected—what was right. Until one day, I found myself pregnant with my third child, so broken and emotionally beat down that I couldn't tell left from right, up from down. My self-esteem, gone. Shot to hell. My head was hung so low I couldn't even look in the mirror without wanting to cry. *Who is this girl?* This broken, tired, wounded version of me? Because I didn't recognize her anymore.

Being pregnant this time had really taken a toll on my body. The miscarriage and the abortions had left my body in a state of complete exhaustion—physically, emotionally, and mentally. I was three months pregnant and desperate for help to escape the hell I was living in—all the lying, the cheating, and yes, the stealing. If he didn't have money and I did, he'd straight-up steal it from me.

I remember one night I was getting ready to head to church for New Year's Eve service. I had to run back to the apartment to grab something and use the bathroom. I rushed into my room and, thinking I was being slick, I tossed my purse into the clothes hamper with the dirty laundry before heading into the bathroom. I knew Ryan didn't have any money—because if he did, he wouldn't have been home. And somehow, this man was *watching me* when I came into the apartment. It was like this motherfucker had x-ray vision or something—like he could see through walls and laundry hampers and shit. I came out of the bathroom just a few minutes later, grabbed my purse from the dirty clothes bin, and headed out the door to church like nothing happened.

Church service had kicked off, the congregation was hyped, folks were catching the spirit, and we were all ready to give our offering—because, you know, sow a little, reap a lot in the New Year, right? You couldn't tell me I wasn't going to reap a harvest after what I had planned to place in that collection plate. I had slid my purse under my seat during service without a second thought. I mean, I was in the Lord's house. Who steals in God's living room?

But when that shiny gold plate lined with red velvet started making its way down the aisle, I reached under to grab my purse, pulled out my wallet, and got ready to give my offering...only to realize something was *off*. Real off. I bet you Satan was somewhere standing nearby, knowing *damn* well what he had made one of his little helpers do—laughing so hard at what he orchestrated, even he couldn't keep his hellish cool. I mean, seriously.

Nothing could've prepared me for what was about to go down. I opened my wallet, ready to give my offering like a good church girl, only to find that *ALL* of my money was gone. Every single dollar. I could've died—*three times*—right there on the spot. Somebody had the nerve to steal my money. *In church!* I sat there like, "What kind of Coney Island, back alley, holy hustle is this?"

I was shocked, upset, and belligerent. I was ready for war right there in the church. So, before I resorted to combat, I sadly took my purse and took my now broke ass home in silent defeat. That whole situation had me *stressed*. *Who steals on New Year's Eve...during church service*? Like, how bold can you be? I couldn't believe it. And all I kept thinking was, *now both of us are going to be broke all year—because ain't no way God is blessing a thief*, especially after they jacked *His* cut! I'm just saying...where's the God in that?!

When I got home, I had made up my mind—I was calling the pastor first thing later that morning to report the holy heist that went down in his sanctuary. Somebody in that church straight-up robbed me, and I wanted my money back *and* a full-blown investigation. This was spiritual robbery, and I was not letting it slide.

I told my friend, who had been at church with me, and she was just as shocked. Her jaw dropped like she'd gotten robbed too. She was right there with me, hyping me up to call the pastor. Honestly, she was so upset you'd think *her* blessing was tied to *my* offering—like we were both about to be stuck in a season of drought because my seed never made it to the plate. No seed, no harvest. Just dry. We were about to be spiritually ashy all year long!

I couldn't wait for morning to come so I could call the pastor and give him the *full* rundown—minute by minute, step by step—from the moment my foot crossed the church doorway. I was ready to break it down like a crime scene investigator. I had timelines. I had details. I was on a mission—and no, it wasn't for discipleship, it was for *deciphering* what the hell happened the moment I slid my bag under that church seat.

Now, here's where it gets good. As I was on the phone venting to my friend about the whole thing—loud, animated, borderline dramatic— somehow, word must've made its way through the walls. Because, to my absolute disbelief, the real thief came forward. And yep, you guessed it—it was Ryan. That evil son-of-a-you-know-what stood there and *boldly* confessed that he had watched me walk in, waited for me to go into the bathroom, then went on a purse hunt like he was on a damn treasure mission. And found it. Case cracked. Holy heist solved.

If I wasn't absolutely terrified of snakes, his ass would've been on a one-way express trip to Coney Island Hospital. But knowing this evil deadbeat, the *snake* probably would've ended up being the real victim—because Ryan was already poisoned with a kind of venom so toxic, it would've made the deadliest snake bite look like a splash of lemon juice. Because I sure as hell would have purchased one and placed it right next to him when he fell asleep. Now you tell me what kind of person does some shit like that?

This evil bastard pulled all kinds of stunts to "keep me in line" or try to control me. And I forgot to mention one of his pettiest, most B.I.T.C.H.-made moves to date. Picture this: I had just spent *hours*—and I mean *HOURS*—getting microbraids in Harlem. If you know NYC, then you *know* getting your hair braided is a full-time job. It's an ALL. DAY. PROCESS. I showed up mad early, sat in that chair from sunup to sundown, and came out looking *flawless*.

I had those braids for maybe a week when Ryan—aka the King of Insecurity—decided he didn't like the idea of me hanging out with my friends at Coney Island Amusement Park. So, what did he do? Grabbed a pair of scissors and started *cutting my braids—with my hair still in them*! I was in absolute shock. It took me the whole weekend to take those things out, one braid at a time, with rage in my heart.

He said something like, "Ain't nobody gonna be looking at *you* with those braids I paid for." And I thought to myself, *Wow—this insecure piece of work is a real B.I.T.C.H.,* emphasis on all the letters. I've always said I think Ryan was born the wrong sex. He did things that only women do when they're past mad—like deep into the land of *pisstivity*. Most men would just walk away, let you cool off, and wait for the storm to pass before trying to talk things out like two civilized human beings.

But not Ryan. Nope. This dude was on a whole different level of petty. He was *so* emotionally reactive and calculated, I used to say he was as predictable as a menstrual cycle on a time clock—regular, moody, and guaranteed to show up with drama. I had never seen Ryan go toe-to-toe with *any* other man the way he loved to square up with me. Not even when his own sister caught a royal black eye, courtesy of her boyfriend. Did he say a word to that man? Nope. Not a single syllable. No, "Hey bro, what the hell?"—nothing. That was the moment I realized: this man was straight-up **P.U.S.S.Y.**

Certified. And that's when it clicked—I had the upper hand. Maybe not in pure muscle, but *oh*, I had him beat in nerve, mouth, and just enough crazy to keep him on edge. I didn't even know I had it in me—but looking back, I definitely saw flashes of it in my dad growing up. My daddy was a certified fool when he got drunk and mad...and guess what? I think I inherited just enough of that wild streak to catch Ryan off guard.

Once I realized I had that "crazy gene," I tapped into it like a secret weapon. And let me tell you—Ryan never saw it coming. During our *last* physical altercation, I beat his ass so good, I shocked *myself*. I pulled strength from somewhere deep down in my soul—so deep it probably had cobwebs. I mean, I went full-on *Muhammad Ali meets Madea* on him. Float like a butterfly, sting like "You got the right one today!"

Getting back to my dad's mean streak—let me tell you about one hot summer weekend. Now, my dad took his weekends *very* seriously, especially when he didn't have to work. That man lived for the weekend like it was a sacred holiday, and he splurged on his alcoholic beverages like there was a statewide drought and only he got the memo. This particular day, there was a baseball game going on, and if you know anything about the South, you know baseball is *a big deal*. Folks treat it like Sunday service. But to me? It was about as exciting as watching paint dry—on a humid day.

My dad, however, had reached that special level of drunk where logic took the day off. And in true "only in my family" fashion, he decided it was the perfect moment to hop on his horse—named after him, naturally—and ride *ole Charlie* straight onto the field. Right up to the pitcher's mound.

You Had to Be There: The Baseball Field Showdown

No one dared—or even had the *nerves*—to step to my dad when he was high as a kite on Kilimanjaro. I mean, the man was a *force to be reckoned with* when he was full of booze. People knew better. So, there he sat, perched proudly atop his horse, Charlie (yes, named after himself), right in the middle of the baseball field—mid-game—like he was the grand marshal of some chaotic Southern parade.

Then, entered one very unfortunate old man.

Now, this guy clearly wasn't from around there. I knew it the moment he walked up to my dad like he had something official to say. Probably thought he was doing a good deed, trying to get the game going again. Bless his brave little heart. I remember the moment like it was yesterday. The man walked right up to my dad and said—brace yourself—**"That's why Martin Luther King is dead."** *I blinked. The world stopped spinning for a second.*

Not only did he not know who **Martin Luther King Jr.** was (at least I *hope* he didn't, or he would have held his peace and waited patiently), he definitely didn't know who **my dad** was. Because if he did? He would've moonwalked backwards off that field, handed someone his hat, and prayed for a second chance at making better life choices.

Some stories don't need exaggeration. This was one of them.

As soon as those words rolled off that old man's tongue, my dad moved like he was the Lone Ranger on a mission. Without skipping a beat, he snatched up the rope he already had in his hand—yes, a *rope*—and tried to **lasso** that man right there on the baseball field.

And let me tell you—*that old man took off!*

He was high-tailing it across that field like his life depended on it (because, let's be real, it kind of did). The whole thing was funny and serious at the same time—one of those moments where you're laughing, but also trying to figure out if you should start praying. I couldn't believe it. My daddy was really out there trying to **rope** a grown man like he was about to enter him in a rodeo. And that's when it hit me—**Daddy was an uncertified nut job.** No license, no paperwork, just vibes.

Right then and there, I realized something:

If alcohol could make somebody act like *that*, it had to be bad for you. No spiritual discernment needed—I just looked at the horse, the rope, and the terrified old man running for his life.

At that time, baby number three was baking in the oven—and let me tell you, *nothing* (and I do mean absolutely **nothing**) had changed between Ryan and me. The cheating wasn't even in the shadows anymore. It was front and center, on full display, and everybody knew about it like it was common neighborhood gossip. At this point, I could feel it—my time in this ten-year, doomed-from-the-start, emotional haunted house was winding down. I just didn't know when or how the door would finally slam shut.

I was four months pregnant. The sun was out, and it was a decent day. I decided to take a walk down Mermaid Avenue to one of the corner stores I used to hit up on the regular—just to clear my mind. And somewhere between the salty breeze and my swollen feet, it hit me: *I'm so done with this fool.* No more pretending. No more excuses. No more "maybe he'll change." So, I did what any emotionally exhausted, pregnant, fed-up woman in Brooklyn would do:

I checked the messages on his beeper—*yep, his beeper*—and listened to every last desperate love note that chick from the neighborhood left him. And just like that... the peace I was trying to hold onto? *Gone.*

Coney Island was small. Like, **nosey neighbor in your business before you even have any** kind of small. If you know anybody, then trust me—**everybody** knows *everything*. There was no hiding. To me, it felt like a recycled mess express. This one messing with that one, that one messing with everyone... just nasty. A real *Jerry Springer starter kit*. So, when I heard that message—the one from *her*—I decided to pop up at the little meetup spot where their "situation" was supposed to go down. And just like that, I found myself in the middle of something I *immediately* regretted. Because there I was, baby in my belly, standing in my insecurity like it was a uniform I couldn't take off. I was ready to fight. I was going to kick that girl's ass—*until I realized it wasn't even about her*. It was about Ryan. And if I'm being real— it wasn't even all his fault either. We were both checked out, drifting in opposite directions, just sharing space and waiting to see who'd pack up first.

However, I couldn't go anywhere. Financially, I was stuck. But emotionally? That day—**those wheels started turning**. Something shifted. And once it did, there was no un-shifting it. That was the beginning of the unraveling. The kind you don't see coming but feel deep down in your gut.

Things got so heated on Mermaid Avenue between that girl and me, the police had to show up—*and so did Ryan*. And the part that burned the most? Watching him shield her. Protect her. Like *she* was the victim. Like I was the one causing chaos in the street while carrying his child. In that moment, my eyes opened all the way up—and baby, I mean *wide open*. And if there had been any part of me still trying to stay asleep in this delusion of a relationship, *that scene right there slapped me all the way into reality*.

My adrenaline was sky high. My tolerance for *any more BS* was at absolute zero. I wasn't about to keep losing myself in that foolishness. So, before I could overthink it—or let guilt trick me into staying again—I packed up my growing belly and my two sweethearts, my babies, and we left. We went straight to a shelter for women of domestic abuse. Because sometimes survival doesn't come with a big dramatic goodbye. Sometimes, it's just a woman saying, *"Enough."*

I had had enough. Of *everything*. The yelling, the cheating, the chaos, the pretending. It was over. I made the decision that my safety—and the safety of my sons—mattered more than staying even *one more minute* in an unhealthy, unstable situation. Because honestly? It was going to go one of two ways: Either I was going to snap and hurt him—*bad*—and end up behind bars, or I was going to survive and save my children. I knew if I let rage take over, I'd lose everything that mattered. And my babies? *They were the reason I had to live, not lose my freedom.*

So, I did the only thing I could. I left. Scared. Alone. Heartbroken. But determined.
I had to be strong for my two sweet boys, even if they were too little to understand what was really happening. All they knew was that everything was different now. No more playground. No more running outside 'til the streetlights came on. No more trips to the beach or long walks on the boardwalk. We weren't in Coney Island anymore—we were in survival mode. But even in that strange, unfamiliar place, I had something I hadn't felt in a long time. **Hope.**

After the intake process with the agency, I was given the place I would now call *home*—at least until I could secure a real one for me and the boys. We were taken to a large house, far from Coney Island. It was spacious, yes—but gloomy. Quiet in that eerie way that matched my mood perfectly. The whole place felt heavy, almost void of life. Like sadness lived there permanently. I was introduced to the woman in charge. We went over a few house rules, and then me and the boys were shown to our room upstairs. It was big—with a bunk bed, a twin bed, and a large dresser. Everything was white: the walls, the blinds, the bedding. Stark. Cold. A blank slate I didn't ask for.

I sat down on the edge of the bed, pulled my babies close, and let the tears fall. I held them tight—tight like a mama bear shielding her cubs from a world they didn't deserve to be thrown into. Then, with the gentlest touch, I felt a small hand wipe away one of my tears.

My sweet seven-year-old looked up at me and asked, **"Mom, what's wrong? Are you alright?"**

I smiled through the ache, looked into their innocent little eyes, and whispered, **"I'm alright."**

Then, I kissed their cheeks like that promise would somehow make it true. I began to settle us into this unfamiliar space, trying not to overwhelm myself with grief—especially now that I was considered a high-risk pregnancy. My body felt heavy. Tired. And I did my best to hide the pain, even though it was written all over me.

After a few hours, me and the boys made our way downstairs to the living room. There was a television and, just to the left, a large kitchen that smelled faintly of cleaning products and something overcooked. I did a quiet sweep of the area, inspecting everything while keeping my babies close, eyes sharp and spirit guarded.

We spent just enough time down there to get a feel for the place before heading back to our room. I watched as my boys looked around—confused, curious, and clearly out of place. There were no long hallways to run through like back at the apartment. No freedom to dash from room to room like they used to. Just one big room that somehow felt *too big* and *too small* all at once. It was large enough to echo but small enough to feel like confinement. And in their little faces, I could see it—this wasn't home. They knew it. *I did too.* I hated seeing them look so confused... so out of place. It tore me to pieces trying to explain to my little ones that Mommy was just trying to build a better life for us—that this was only temporary.

But how could they understand? How could they possibly know that their mommy was carrying years of pain, heartbreak, and silent battles? That I had reached a place where I didn't even want to exist anymore...And yet— they were the reason I still did. They were my lifeline.

My tether to this side of heaven. But how do you explain something like that to a seven-year-old and to a four-year-old whose biggest worry should be snack time and cartoons? You don't.

You just hold them a little tighter and hope your strength speaks louder than your brokenness.

My oldest knew. There was a level of maturity in him at such a young age that I couldn't fully explain. It was like he'd been here before—like he had this quiet understanding of the world that went beyond his years. He became my blanket of comfort. He looked after his little brother, made sure he was okay— like he knew I didn't have much left to give, and he stepped in without even being asked.

Soon after settling in, I met two other women in the shelter—both with children of their own—and we quickly grew close. We looked out for each other, leaned on each other, and built a little village right there in that broken space. Our kids got along like they'd known each other forever, and so did we. We cooked together, had dinner together, swapped stories, and cried over shared pain. We laughed when we could and held each other up when we couldn't. We were close—closer than I ever expected to be with strangers. They had my back. They took care of me and my babies like we were their own. They became my sisters. The family I didn't know I'd find... so far from home.

I never called my family to tell them what had happened. I couldn't. I was too ashamed to admit that I had made a terrible mistake going back—back to *him*, back to the chaos, back to the monster I thought might change. Only God and the few people in my life *there* knew what my world had become. What I had endured and what I was still surviving.

As my pregnancy progressed, so did the dangerous conditions of carrying this precious gift. I had no amniotic fluid. My gynecologist told me I had two options: terminate the life growing inside me or wait for a spontaneous abortion to happen on its own. I was confused. I had no connection to God at the time. I was a complete basket case, unraveling by the minute. I took my doctor's advice. Reluctantly, a few days later, I called an abortion clinic to schedule the demise of my unborn child. Just saying that out loud hurt. I cried. I saw other women in the neighborhood expecting—smiling, glowing, planning. I wondered how they felt waiting to meet their babies. And me, I was devastated. Completely undone.

I cried out to God, saying, "Why do they get to have their babies... and I have to lose mine?" It wasn't fair.

I cried some more.

And then... the day came. It was a day I had to make my way into the city, walking straight into the weight of what became the most dreaded decision of my life. My friend Janet was with me for support—just like she always had been. We arrived hours before I was scheduled to go through with the abortion.

I was sitting there, lost in deep thought, whispering to myself, "I can't do this again. I don't want to do this." Patient after patient was called. The list was getting shorter. My name was next. I felt it in my chest—the panic, the heartbreak, the weight of it all. And just like that, I gently pulled myself up from the lobby chair...and walked out.

I felt a wave of calm rush over me—a deep, quiet relief that came with the decision I had made. I wasn't going to end my pregnancy. I was going to see it through, even if it killed me. And honestly? It came close. *Extremely* close to killing me. The amniotic fluid continued to drop. I started seeing flashes of light. My body began to swell—*double in size*—as fluid built up faster than it could be released. Everything felt heavy. Slow. Dangerous.

Eventually, I was placed on strict bed rest. Then came another dreaded decision—one that shattered me in a whole different way. I had to release the boys into Ryan's custody until I gave birth. I had no other choice. My body was breaking down, and I couldn't care for them the way they needed. It broke my heart, but I knew it was the only way I had a shot at bringing my baby into the world—and making it back myself.

I was moved to a downstairs bedroom in the shelter, which made things a little easier on my very swollen, very over-it body. I was bouncing from appointment to appointment, trying to make sure both the baby and I were at least *somewhat* stable. Nothing about my situation felt steady, but I was trying. During that time, I started calling on God more than ever. Like, *nonstop*. He seemed to be listening too—making a way for me and the boys little by little. I prayed so much and so often, I'm sure God was like, *"Okay, beloved... I got you the first forty times. Go lie down. Take a nap. Let Me work. I'll circle back."* But what can I say? I was desperate, tired, and *extra holy* in that season.

Isn't it peculiar how a serious situation will drop you straight to your knees, praying like your life depends on it? (*Because it usually does.*) I always wondered why, once the storm passes, we tend to call on God a little less—until the next hurdle shows up waving at us from a distance. I hated that about myself. I always have.

Since then, I try to be consistent, steady in my prayers, keeping that line of communication open. But truth be told, I find myself slipping—forgetting His goodness, forgetting all the countless times He's pulled me out of messes I had no business overcoming. Sticky situations, divine rescues, grace on top of grace...and somehow, I still forget. Working on that. For real.

Now back to my scary moment. My amniotic fluid began to increase as the pregnancy progressed. I was a wonder to doctors as they had never seen a case such as my pregnancy. They were caring and made sure I received the best medical attention they could possibly give to me and my unborn. Ryan even *seemed* concerned enough to be involved—to check in on me, ask questions, pretend to care. But all that changed the day we had a conversation about life insurance.

The details of that day are a bit blurry now, but what I do remember—clear as day—is lying in that hospital bed, barely hanging on, my body no longer able to keep up with carrying the little joy growing inside me. Then, I overheard Ryan ask the insurance agent, *"If the baby doesn't make it, will the insurance still be approved?"*

That was it. I was furious. Beyond furious. I was hurt, sick, pregnant, and sitting in a hospital bed with the man who was supposed to care about us asking about a payout instead of praying for a heartbeat. That moment flipped a switch in me. And honestly? I believe it flipped one in my body too. Because not long after he left the hospital, everything in me began to spiral. My vitals shot up. My organs started acting out—functioning in ways that were dangerously unpredictable.

My body had had enough. And now... so had I. The nurses were watching me like a hawk—taking blood every hour, checking my urine, monitoring every single thing. It was nonstop attention, and the more they hovered, the more scared I became. I tried not to cry, but I couldn't help it. The fear was too real.

A few hours after Ryan left, my doctor came in with the news: the baby had to come out.

My body had officially entered the danger zone—**preeclampsia.** But thanks to Ryan's lovely little insurance conversation, my blood pressure had skyrocketed. I was way too unstable to risk surgery. The chances of both of us not making it were too high. So, we had to wait—wait for my body to calm down, wait for my vitals to settle. Wait and pray.

The delivery was happening. No more delays. My baby was coming early—ready or not—at just thirty-two weeks. On October 22, 1998, my tiny bundle of joy came into the world, weighing just 5 lbs. A preemie. He was the cutest little thing I had ever seen at that size. His head was the size of the palm of my hand. How could someone so tiny have caused such a terrifying pregnancy? But the moment I laid eyes on him, all that chaos and craziness became a blur. None of it mattered. All I wanted in that moment was my family. I didn't know what the future held for me and my three babies. What I did know was this: I had just been discharged from the shelter... and now, I was back with Ryan and his family in that same apartment in Coney Island. I felt I had taken one hundred steps backwards.

However, all wasn't lost. I had gotten approved for an apartment while all this madness was unfolding in my life, but I had to find it on my own. I searched and searched all over for a decent place and neighborhood for me and the boys. It was exhausting, but God provided me the strength to do so. I was desperate. I was determined. I was a woman on a mission.

I prayed. I got serious with God, praying specific requests. I said, "Lord, I want to live in a nice neighborhood. I want to live on the first floor. I want an apartment that is spacious." Guess what? HE gave me what I asked Him for. And from that day on, I knew God heard me. I knew He was real. And I knew that when you draw close to Him, He will draw close to you—not that He's far to begin with. It's us who stray far away from Him.

Here's what happened next—and it may shock you... or maybe not. **I. Tried. To. Make. It. Work. With. Ryan. AGAIN.** Yes, you heard me. My boys needed a father in their life—or so I thought. Just like I had needed my father. I was living in my own apartment, across town, far enough away from Coney Island. I was in Crown Heights, Brooklyn—and God really came through on *every* detail of my prayer.

Today, Crown Heights is one of the most expensive sections of Brooklyn to live in—but back then, it was home. My children had access to multiple parks to play in, and they were just happy to finally be in a place we could truly call our own. They had their own bedrooms—what more could kids ask for at their age, especially after everything we'd been through? I don't know what made me think that things might be different because that we had our own place. **What a foolish thought.**

As I settled into our new space, I started to feel something I hadn't felt in a long time—**safe. Independent. Free.** But Ryan? He hadn't changed one bit. Still the same evil, vindictive person he had always been. And the more comfortable I became in my own space, the more I could feel myself breaking free from the grip he had on me all those years. It wasn't until I was on winter recess from my job and went back home to Mississippi with the boys that I had an epiphany—my very real *Ah-hah!* moment. I was **DONE.**

It took a visit home for me to finally get real with myself and begin the work on *me*—to let go of the baggage that had weighed me down for far too long. My family still didn't know everything I had been through—all those years later, I was still carrying it alone. I wished they lived closer so my brothers could've put a whooping on that motherfucker for every time he felt the need to lay hands on me. I wished I could've told my dad all the horrible things Ryan had done. But I didn't. I stayed silent. Broken. Alone in my pain. And I still wondered—what would my dad have done? Would he have even cared? God, I wish he knew how much I needed him to come to my aid.

I returned to New York and walked into my beautiful apartment, surrounded by my beautiful little boys—my family, my peace. I walked into my bedroom, looked Ryan straight in the eye, and told him he had to go. "I can't do this anymore." Just like that, I felt the weight lift. The heaviness that had lived on my chest for years was gone. All those years of physical and mental abuse were finally getting the boot—and this time, *I* wasn't on the receiving end of it.

For the very first time in my life, I let out a sigh of relief—and it felt damn good.

Freeing. Liberating. Long overdue.

♥ 1 Corinthians 13:4–7 (ESV)

4 "Love is patient and kind; love does not envy or boast; it is not arrogant

5 or rude. It does not insist on its own way; it is not irritable or resentful;

6 it does not rejoice at wrongdoing, but rejoices with the truth.

7 Love bears all things, believes all things, hopes all things, endures all things."

Just when light was finally starting to shine through the pitch-black tunnel of my life—and Ryan and I were completely **OVER**—things took a turn. A sharp, unexpected turn. One that put me on a path I wouldn't wish on my *worst* enemy. Do you remember when I told you Ryan should've been born female, the way he carried on? Always doing things only women are *stereotypically* known to do when they're hurt or bitter? Well, he took that to a whole new level.

He became the woman scorned. Not me. Honestly, why *should* I feel scorned? I was the one trying to escape his grip. But apparently—it turns out—I must've had a grip on him too.

As crazy as it sounds, I couldn't believe his next move to try and control me—even away from him—with me living my life, free from his chaos, with him nowhere in it, except to see the boys. I was never one of those bitter women who kept the father from seeing his kids. *Nope. Not me.* I was smarter than that. I needed a break—some *me time.* Time to breathe, to be with myself, to laugh with friends and feel like a person again. So, every weekend, the boys would head out to Coney Island to spend time with him.

It worked for all of us... or so I thought. Just when I thought my relationship with Ryan couldn't get any worse. One Friday after work, I went to pick up the kids from him like usual, ready to head home and just relax, enjoy the weekend with them. But the boys wanted to stay in Coney Island—nothing new. I was fine with it, just like all the other times. And Ryan usually was too. But apparently, he must've been on his cycle that day, because out of nowhere he decided he didn't want the boys to stay with him that weekend. Like he suddenly needed to block whatever he assumed *I* had going on.

When he told me no, I didn't argue. I simply picked up the phone in the kitchen to call his niece and ask if she'd be willing to keep the boys for the weekend instead. And just as I was ending the call with her—**Ryan hit me across the face.** And that was it. I snapped. I went into full-blown **attack mode**. He ran—to get away from me—and the boys heard the commotion and came running to where I was.

Ryan had shoved the baby stroller between us like it was a shield, keeping me from getting to him and completely *messing his world up.* And trust me— I was ready to. So instead, I took my older sons and left. I went to Ryan's sister's apartment and waited there until his mom got home so I could get my baby and go home with my children. But while I was waiting at her place, there was a knock at the door. **It was the cops.** Yep—*you guessed it.* Ryan called the police and lied. What exactly he said, God only knows. But whatever it was, it was enough to get me arrested. Even though I protested. Even though I told them the truth—that *he* had laid hands on *me.* It didn't matter. They cuffed me anyway.

The damage was done and the officer said, he called first and they had to take me in being that it was a domestic dispute. I could not believe what was happening. I was in shock. That was the ultimate bitch move, and it was clear he was the pussy I had believed he was all those years. He would never step to a male the way he always stepped to me to abuse me.

I was taken to the precinct and placed in a small cell while being booked and prepped for transfer to central booking in downtown Brooklyn. I waited and waited. The whole process felt endless. Then, the arresting officer came over and told me something I couldn't believe—Ryan had actually shown up to the precinct to drop the charges. But the officer told him it was too late. He said, "I know he's lying, but once the call is made and we show up, we have to take someone in." I thought that was straight-up **bullshit**. So, there I was— going to jail for something I didn't even do. I was taken downtown. The next thing I knew I was sitting in a cell with a group of other women who had also been booked. I remember **freezing**—shivering from how cold it was in there. Not just physically, but emotionally cold. Alone. Angry. Tired. And still trying to process how I got there in the first place.

I remember one female officer judging me like she had any clue what I had been through. She didn't know a damn thing about my story, my pain, or the hell I had endured for years. And yet, there she was, throwing stones from her little glass badge. I looked at her with nothing but **disdain**. As I sat on that cold bench, my head in my lap, I felt... nothing. Void of life. Void of feeling. Void of emotion. I wasn't even afraid at that point. *Afraid of what?* What more could be taken from me?

Then this one woman—another detainee—looked over at me and said, **"Whatever they got you in here for, I know you didn't do it."** She didn't know me from a can of paint, and yet she saw what that officer couldn't—*my truth.* She saw past the cuffs, past the silence, past the judgment. And I laughed—really laughed—when she said it. Something about her words, the way she said it... it brought me a little peace in that moment. A sense of relief. And right then, I knew **I was going to be alright.** I spent the entire weekend in that place.

By Monday, I was finally assigned an attorney, and she was so kind to me. Even she said she could tell I was innocent and couldn't understand why the officer hadn't arrested Ryan, too. I just shrugged my shoulders and answered every question she asked. What else could I do?

When I was released, I was *so* glad to be out of there and back in my own little world of freedom. But things just kept getting worse. I lost my job and had to spend months going back and forth to criminal court. Eventually, the case was dropped and I got my job back.

This time, I was a woman on a mission. And no devil in hell was going to stop me. I threw myself into bettering me and giving my sons nothing but the best. I had to attend Family Court—fighting for full custody and child support. At that point, I'd been to court so often that I had developed a rapport with a few of the Court Officers—we were on a first-name basis. I even got invited to one of their annual Christmas parties. I remember one of them asking me, "How in the hell did *you* end up with somebody like Ryan?" I laughed it off, but deep down, it was almost embarrassing to be asked that—especially by other men who clearly saw what I couldn't. A total loser.

I had been in court so long, and had done so much on my own, that when I finally had to obtain an attorney to get a conviction for nonpayment of child support, the attorney looked at me and said, **"You've already done everything I would've done. You've been doing this pro se all these years."** That's how good I had gotten at representing myself. Truth be told, I barely needed a lawyer. But still—the court's rulings, when it came to getting support, were always *unfavorable.* His consequences? A slap on the wrist—*if that.*

Ryan chose to quit his job—*on purpose*—just so he wouldn't have to pay to take care of his children. And here I am, years later, writing this book, and I'm still owed over **$100,000** in child support arrears. Ryan is still out here dodging responsibility, avoiding real work, and beating the system—*even now,* with my boys grown into young men. And no—I still haven't shared any of this with my family. Not even my dad.

"That which does not kill us makes us stronger."

FRIEDRICH NIETZSCHE

6
RELATIONSHIP #2: MARCUS
Girl, what's wrong with you? From the frying pan to the fire... Why do you keep doing this?

ow did I end up in *another* disastrous relationship—this time with a man even more abusive than the last? I wish I could say it was just a nightmare, something I'd eventually wake up from. But no, it was real. And I was knee-deep in it. I had finally worked up the courage to escape the hell I'd been living in with my children's father. I was trying to move forward, to rebuild, to breathe.

Away from him.

Away from the suffocating weight of it all.

Away from the sickening scent of the Atlantic Ocean that hit me every time I returned from visiting family in Mississippi—reminding me I was walking back into a familiar kind of pain.

The urine-stained elevators.

The cold, bitter winds coming off the water.

The winters that felt like punishment.

Coney Island had stopped feeling like home a long time ago.

I was in a new environment now—a new neighborhood, far enough away that nothing reminded me of life on that little island where everybody knew everybody. I had met Marcus back when I was still living in Coney Island. He wasn't what you'd call handsome—but what he lacked in looks, he made up for with his goofy antics. He kept me laughing with all the ridiculous things he'd do just for a chuckle or a little attention. I thought he was cool to hang out with, harmless fun. But never—not even for a minute—did I think he'd be someone I'd be interested in, let alone involved with. But what did I really know about love or healthy relationships? Let's be honest—I didn't have the best track record. I'd already gone down that road before, and we all know how that ended. So, when Marcus found out I lived nearby and just *popped up* at my door one day...I was completely caught off guard. Speechless, really. Because here we go again.

It was a Saturday afternoon. I was home, just relaxing in bed, when there was a knock at the door. I opened it—and there he was. Marcus. Standing there with that devilish grin on his face like he was up to something. Looking back, I *should've* taken that moment as a warning—a sign that something bad was hovering right outside my door, looking for a way in to flip my world upside down. But no. I opened the door. I let him in. And from that day on, we started hanging out. One thing led to another, and before I knew it, I was knee-deep in a short but *tumultuous* relationship. It only took me three years to learn my lesson. **Three years.** Let me tell you—when you're going through hell, three years feels like *forever*.

In the beginning, Marcus was fun to be around. He was always inviting me out, taking me places—though, truth be told, most of them weren't really my scene. He and I were total opposites when it came to the kind of people we hung around. I'm the shy, reserved type—quiet, lowkey, not one for the spotlight, but Marcus was loud, bold, and always needed to be seen and heard. Naturally, he gravitated toward places and people that matched that energy.

At first, it all felt a little adventurous. He was pulling me out of my comfort zone, introducing me to new experiences and people—including some pretty well-known names in the rap industry. I'll admit, it was exciting. Fun, even. And through those connections, I met a few people who ended up becoming real blessings in my life. My girl Adrianna, with her bubbly, full-of-life energy that I absolutely love—and Dax, too. To this day, those two are still in my life.

And no matter what happens, they always will be. I don't remember exactly when Marcus started showing me a different side of himself—one I hadn't seen before. He drank beer regularly, but at first, he seemed to have it under control. He didn't come across as sloppy or out of his mind, so I assumed he could handle it. But looking back, I should've known—anyone who drinks beer like it's a replacement for water has a problem.

I overlooked it. And that oversight cost me—*big time.* By the time I realized how deep his dependency went, it was too late. The monster had already stepped out from behind the dark curtain... and moved into my home. Right there—with me and my children. Sometimes, it was hard to tell when he was sober and when he wasn't. His two personalities started to blur. But I had watched him enough to learn the difference. There was **Marcus**—the fun, hyperactive guy who kept me laughing. And then there was **Marcus**—the controlling, unpredictable, abusive man I learned to fear.

It got to the point where I didn't even enjoy being out in public with Marcus anymore. He had become a walking embarrassment—constantly accusing someone of trying to talk to me, even when no one was paying me the slightest bit of attention. His rants were exhausting and always out of pocket. I remember one particular moment that still sticks with me. We were at a gas station, and a group of guys had pulled up on their motorcycles. I thought it was the coolest thing—their club gear, the sound of the engines, the way they rode those powerful machines like they owned the city streets.

As they pulled into the station, my eyes locked on one bike in particular. It was orange and silver—unlike anything I'd ever seen before. Sleek, bold, beautiful. I couldn't stop staring. Not at the rider—**at the bike.** Marcus knew I loved motorcycles. He knew that. But when he caught me looking in that direction, his whole mood flipped. He went **ballistic** yelling at the top of his lungs. Marcus shouted, **"What the fuck—you want that nigga on the bike?"**

His voice cut through the air, loud and reckless. He was so out of control, I truly thought he was about to go confront the guy—some poor man who didn't even know I existed. My neighbor, who was sitting in the back seat with us, had to calm him down. He was just as shocked as I was by Marcus's behavior. That day, I made a decision. I didn't get back in his car.

I stayed home. It was safer. It was quieter. And honestly, it was just less *dramatic* to stay home and get lost in a good book—where the only chaos came from fiction, not my front seat.

It bothered Marcus that I chose solitude over spending time with him. But one good thing did come out of it—he started paying attention to my love for reading. He'd ask what authors I liked. He'd bring books home for me, or call and ask if I wanted something by a particular writer. It was one of the very few thoughtful things he did. Not all of the three years with Marcus were terrible. He was the kind of person who would put his whole heart into making someone smile. He loved doing things that were fun, exciting, and over-the-top—especially on special occasions. On Valentine's Day and Christmas, he went above and beyond to make those days feel extra special, and I genuinely appreciated that side of him. **It was when he wasn't drinking** and when he wasn't so far gone that he'd lose focus and start acting impulsive, reckless, or just plain foolish.

I'll give him this—he did have a soft spot for my boys. He'd take them to the park, teach them how to play checkers, and even plan little outings. I remember them going to 42nd Street, riding the big Ferris wheel inside the Toys-R-Us store. Those were the moments that made me want to believe in him, the moments that made me hope the good in him could somehow outweigh the bad. He was good to the boys. But they weren't blind. They saw how he treated me—how his behavior shifted—and they didn't like it. And deep down, I knew it, too.

I had made another mistake. I had let someone into my life who thought using his hands was a way to control me—as if I needed to be reprimanded like a child, and *he* was the one to do it, even when there was no reason. Not that there ever **is** a reason—because let's be clear:

There is never an excuse to put your hands on someone.

Not out of anger. Not out of control. Not ever.

No grown woman—or man—should ever accept abuse from anyone. And yet, there I was trying to hold together what I already knew was broken. As time went on, I became more and more dissatisfied in the relationship. Something in me—*that womanly intuition*—started going off. Little things Marcus did or said started raising red flags. I began asking questions. And, of course, he denied everything. Every. Single. Time. But then I found a sheet of notebook paper—covered in phone numbers. *A lot* of them. That's when the suspicion really kicked in. I started connecting the dots and had a strong feeling Marcus had been hanging around the high school up the block—*and not for any good reason.*

He started becoming harder to reach, disappearing here and there with no real explanation. Then, I found provocative pictures of him with some girl in Atlantic City. And of course, just like clockwork, he tried to convince me she meant nothing. Another lie. Another excuse. There were times I'd ask him to leave—*and then turn right around and let him back in.*

It was a cycle, a draining, depressing cycle. And I was tired of going through the same tired nonsense over and over again. When I asked him to leave, he fought me. He forced himself on me, thinking that sex would somehow change my mind—as if violating me would make me stay. It was not consensual. **It was rape.**

There was one time I called the cops after he hit me and tried to trap me inside my bedroom, refusing to let me leave the apartment. When the police arrived, it wasn't just one or two officers—there were seven cops inside my apartment, questioning both of us like we were equals in the chaos. They listened to our stories, pieced together what they could. When it was all said and done, one of the officers turned to both of us. His eyes locked on me, and he said, **"If we have to come back here again, we're taking both of you in."** Just like that. No protection. No justice. Just a warning that felt more like a threat—directed at the wrong person. I was in shock—total disbelief at what the officer had just said. *Me?* The one being attacked in my own home? The one trying to escape a controlling monster with a drinking problem? Somehow, *we both* would be locked up—for something I had no power to stop.

It broke my heart. **Once again, the system had failed me.** And I wasn't about to let it happen a second time. I had already been put through the system before—by my children's father.

He was the abuser.

He called the police.

He lied.

And the only explanation I was ever given was that he called first—*even though he was the aggressor all along.*

I was barely 5'3" to his 6'1" frame and you believed him. No way was this happening a second time. I had to figure something out and fast. I was not going to allow this monster to ever hit, rape, control, and endanger me of losing my children. I had to be smart about things going forward. So, I began to pray to God, and I prayed a prayer that only He could answer.

Marcus was still living with me. I was miserable, and he knew it. It had taken a toll on me mentally and physically. I saw all the signs, and his mother had warned me about him. I liked his mother because she shot straight from the hip. He knew that about her, and he was very disrespectful towards her, calling her the B word on many occasions when she was not falling for his bullshit. She was old school, and she knew what she had as a son, but I guess God allowed her to see me as someone she could advise to not go down or should I say continue to go down that road of destruction with her son. However, I did not heed her warnings but found out the very hard way by experiencing what she wanted me to avoid. I can tell you, experience is the best teacher, but if you can bypass it do so because you will not like the consequences it brings in the lessons you miss or fail to learn. Why I failed to listen to the warnings of others looking from the outside is beyond me. Was I so blinded by wanting to be accepted that I chose the poorest? I recall taking Marcus home with me to meet my family. My sister informed me some time later that her husband, my brother-in-law, said to her that Marcus beats me. I guess men know other men and what's inside them even when women like me fail to see what is actually underneath the layers. Even other men from my neighborhood would ask why was I with that fool. Of course, this was after we had separated. They would say he was no good for you and he didn't deserve me because I was too pretty and nice to be with someone like him. So, I asked, why didn't you ask or say these things to me when I was with him? I probably would have accepted the gesture and ended the relationship sooner. Maybe hearing it come from another man's mouth would have been welcomed, I don't know. I wondered why men just sat back and watch Marcus' bullshit unfold in my life and just kept silent. I could not understand that. Men that I considered father figures asked me why I was with him and that I deserved better. I would have listened intently to their advice and ended it, had this conversation taken place.

Marcus had almost succeeded at ending my life when he was asked to leave because I did not want to continue in the hell he called a relationship. In his rage, he held me down on the bed and began choking me. I could not breathe nor speak, and I saw my life slipping away at that moment, everything was slowly turning dark, I could sense my eyes closing, and then he let go. I lay there motionless, and I wanted to cry because I could only think of the unthinkable. My boys could have been motherless. I couldn't show weakness for that monster to feed on, so I continued to lie there. I was tired of the bite marks he left on both sides of my cheeks whenever he felt that I was his territory, and I needed to be branded. I was tired of the numerous women calling, the evidence of pictures, or neighbors informing me. Then, seeing it for myself when he and my neighbor who pretended to be a friend had gone to his house and he had his way with her and took pictures that I happened to find. I was done, and enough was enough with the role I played in allowing him to do these things to me. My boys deserved better even if I felt I was not deserving because I felt like I couldn't do better than the two cowards I had allowed to come into my life and steal my joy and peace and even tried to steal my breath of life. I was done with the devil and he had to go. So, I prayed and asked God to open up a door for Marcus to leave, and I promised I would not open it for him to come back in. God answered. I kept my promise. I learned the lesson this time around. It was hard and painful, but I learned. The next lesson nothing could have prepared me for.

7

RELATIONSHIP #3: Stan

Never Say Never

It was October 2004, and I've found myself knee-deep in yet another horrible relationship that I was desperately trying to crawl out of—preferably without losing what little sanity I had left. I hated being stuck in that frustrating rerun of abuse, like some twisted TV series where the script never changed, just different characters, a new villain in the leading male role, and the lead actress (me) refusing to walk off set. I couldn't figure out why I kept making such poor choices when it came to men. Then one day, I heard Oprah say, *"You attract who you are."* And let me tell you, the moment those words left her mouth, I was ready to throw a shoe at the screen. I rolled my eyes so hard; I almost saw my childhood. I wanted to argue with her, passionately—because I considered myself a good person. But deep down, I couldn't help but wonder if there was some inconvenient truth in her statement. I mean, I considered myself a good person—kind, loving, loyal, and an amazing cook! Surely I wasn't attracting these emotionally bankrupt men because of *who I was*.

But the words stuck. They kept buzzing around in my brain like an annoying fly I couldn't swat away. Maybe it wasn't about me being *bad*, but maybe, just maybe, it was about what I believed I deserved. That was a hard truth to sit with. I started noticing my internal dialogue. I realized I had been carrying invisible baggage with broken handles: childhood trauma, low self-esteem, and a trunk full of unhealed wounds dressed up as independence. And every time I thought I had packed light, I was unknowingly checking in a full suitcase of emotional triggers.

I began to ask myself the questions I had been avoiding, *Why do I keep inviting pain to the party of my life? Why do I settle for the uncomfortable and the chaos than peace?* The more I wrestled with these questions, the more I began to understand—healing had to start with me. The truth is, I was ready to attract someone good, but first I had to make peace. I still saw love as something I had to earn, fight for, or survive through. That wasn't love—it was emotional gymnastics, and I was stuck in a routine I hadn't even choreographed.

But that season marked the beginning of a shift. I didn't magically become a new person overnight (I'm not that good), but I started seeing myself through the lens of grace instead of guilt. I took Oprah's words and gave them context—they weren't an accusation. They were an invitation to look inward. When I finally did, I discovered the most important relationship I had neglected: the one with myself. This was my aha moment, and I fully understood what Oprah meant, so I was on a mission to change me if I was to stop those cycles of bad relationships with men who were broken just like me. That wasn't the ending. It was the plot twist I didn't see coming, the kind that made me want to keep reading... even if I was a little scared of what the next words in the chapter held.

I had been in a minor car accident and was going to therapy to ease the tension I'd been feeling in my neck and back. Three days a week, a driver was sent to take me to and from the medical facility in the evenings. Normally, I was super alert in the presence of strangers—always on guard, always reading the room—but on this particular day, I was too worn out from work to pay attention to anything or anyone. I was just relieved that I didn't have to drive myself. So, when my driver pulled up, I politely hopped in the back seat and zoned out as we made our way—me and a few other clients—to the clinic for physical therapy. It was during my second visit that I really took notice—and let me tell you, I was intrigued by what I saw. The guy was *handsome*. Not the "maybe he's cute if I squint" kind of handsome, but the "whoa, where have you been hiding?" kind. From the back seat, I found myself suddenly distracted, my therapist-bound thoughts replaced with something far less clinical. And just like that, a question snuck into my mind, bold and uninvited: *What would it be like to be in a relationship with him?*

Naturally, I began my silent investigation—glancing at his left hand for that telltale ring. No ring. I perked up a little. *Okay,* I thought, *he's definitely not off-limits.* But I quickly reeled it in. *No ring doesn't necessarily mean he's single—it could mean divorced, separated, allergic to commitment, or just one of those people who conveniently "forgets" to wear it.* Still, my curiosity was piqued, and there was no turning back. Then, I noticed (in the dash) a picture of a baby girl. *Well,* I said to myself, *that's one question answered—he has a child.* Before I realized what was happening, I had secretly developed a crush on this man, and I didn't know him from a can of paint. He was like a mystery to me, and I suddenly wanted to know more about him. I didn't know why I was feeling those things toward a stranger I had just met. There was something about him—maybe the calm way he drove, or the way he carried himself—that grabbed my attention without even trying. And there I was, in the back seat, trying to piece together clues about a man I hadn't even said two words to yet.

I was still in a dead relationship with Marcus that needed to be buried once and for all, so I patiently waited because I knew it was quickly coming to a close, but I just didn't know when or how. I did know that it was probably going to be messy because that's how Marcus handled all his bullshit, MESSY! I'd been going to therapy for about a month, and by that time, I'd learned my driver's name—Stan—through casual small talk on our rides to the facility. Somewhere along the way, I graduated from the back seat to riding shotgun. That was mostly because he decided I should be his first pick-up of the evening, and I wasn't mad at it.

One day, we were sitting in the car waiting for his second passenger to come out, and that's when we started talking more—really talking. And I don't know what came over me, but I opened up to Stan like the Red Sea opened up for Moses. Just parted ways with all my emotional baggage and let it pour out. There was something about him—his energy, his calmness, the way he listened without interrupting—that made it feel safe to speak freely. And I did. I let it all flow, like I was at a free therapy session before even getting to the therapy session. Now, don't get me wrong—I wasn't trying to throw myself at this man. But something about Stan made me feel seen. Not in a "he's-staring-at-me" way, but in that rare "I hear you even when you don't say a word" kind of way. It was unnerving... and refreshing. He nodded at the right times, smiled when I needed it, and chuckled when I threw in a sarcastic comment to lighten the emotional load. That's when I realized I wasn't just enjoying the ride to therapy—I was looking forward to it.

Therapy was still doing what it needed to do for my neck and back, but that ride to and from the facility? That was where my spirit was getting some unexpected healing. I told him about the horrible relationship I was in—well, the one I was *trying* to get out of. He listened intently, no interruptions, no judgment, just that same calm energy that always made the car feel like a safe space. Then he said, "You're too nice and too pretty to be involved with someone who doesn't respect you." And just like that, he called Marcus what I had long suspected but never said out loud—weak. "Any man who feels he needs to put his hands on a woman is a weak person," he said plainly, like it was just common sense, which it *should've* been. Then he hit me with, "You're a beautiful woman. You don't need to be with someone who's not treating you right." Now, don't get me wrong—I already knew this before Marcus and I even crossed the line from casual to complicated. Stan wasn't telling me anything brand new; he was just confirming what my gut had been screaming for a while. And sometimes, confirmation from the front seat of a green minivan hits different. At this point, Stan and I were just acquaintances and the thought of being in a relationship had settled within me but I was still attracted to him. No, it wasn't a sexual attraction, that never entered my mind. It was as if I was smitten by him and he had no idea. As the months rolled by, the answer to my prayer was finally granted—Marcus was history. It was a new year, and I was looking forward to discovering where this newfound freedom from abuse would take me. I was cautious, sure, but I was also intentional. I stayed mindful of my thoughts, focused on keeping my mindset positive, and gave myself permission to just stop and smell the roses for once. After spending fifteen long years inhaling the toxic fumes of two relationships with men who had no business occupying space in my life, I was done. I knew I couldn't get that time back, and yes, that stung—but I was going to make the most of what I had left. I was determined to pour my energy into my boys, focus on myself, and grow in my career. It was time for me.

It was getting late, and Stan was about to take me and two other passengers home. As we're waiting for the traffic light to turn green, Stan looked over at me and said, "I'm trying to decide who I should drop home first." Then, he asked, "Can I kidnap you?" My heart fluttered. *Did I hear him correctly?* I immediately thought to myself. Of course, I heard him correctly because my insides were jumping with joy because I really liked him, and if my heart could have smiled it would have been because it was happy too. *Is he interested in me?* I asked myself. *Is this his way of making it known.* The girl with the crush on him wanted to say, *Hell, yes! Kidnap me. I ain't got nothing to do, nowhere to be, and besides no one would look for me if I were kidnapped.* However, I stayed reserved, and the lady inside responded, "I don't mind taking the drive with you." I knew he was interested because I only lived about six miles from the medical office, and the other passengers lived much further, in Coney Island. If that wasn't obvious that he was interested, I don't know what could have made it any clearer than him just coming right out and saying it. I could not believe what was happening to me, and I was enjoying every minute of it. That handsome guy was interested in me, the girl whose self-esteem was almost non-existent, the girl who thought of herself as too unattractive to get someone like Stan to notice her or even show interest. But he noticed, and I was slowly breaking those self-destructive thoughts that had plagued my mind for so many years by men who felt that way about themselves but projected it on me to believe the same about myself.

After dropping off the two passengers, we drove to the arcade a few blocks away in Coney Island. We played a few games, had small talk, and he drove me home. As we sat and talked for a few moments, he leaned in and kissed me ever so gently. I exited the vehicle excited. What came next took me by total surprise. I had always said that I would never do something, especially if it was wrong and was against my moral values. Being involved with a married man was one thing I said I would never do because I saw firsthand what it could do to a marriage as I had seen with my parents. I didn't want that done to me nor do that to any woman. So, when Stan told me that he was married and had children I was disappointed because I assumed that for the first time, I had found someone who I could enhance my happiness with. He had the qualities that I longed for in my past relationships. He was easy to talk to, very attentive, and he showed a genuine interest in getting to know me.

As time went on, our relationship grew and he proved to be all that I had assumed he was. It was like meeting the male version of myself. He would say what I was thinking, and oftentimes we would complete each other's sentences. However, the choice I made went against everything I knew was morally wrong, disappointing, and displeasing to God. I chose wrong over right and took the hand of Satan and went down that road of adultery. I struggled with that choice early on in that relationship, but I became numb to it over the six years of my involvement with him until that dreadful day in May 2011.

As time passed, I waited to see a change in Stan as I had seen in the past two relationships I was in with Ryan and Marcus. Six months no change. Year one no change. I thought this was too good to be true. The more I didn't see change, the more I fell in love with him. Not the kind of love you have in the beginning but wears off after getting to know the person. I loved him with my whole heart, my soul. I wasn't in love with him, I truly loved him with everything that was within me. It was genuine. It was without fear. It was without abuse, so I told myself. But who was I kidding? The devil can have you so blinded that you can ride on the edge of a cliff, and all you see are the beautiful clouds and not the dead drop below.

I was so badly wounded from my past relationships that I could barely let Stan come near me without physically putting up my guards. I recall, on numerous occasions, when we would be sitting in his car, and Stan would reach over to kiss me, I would flinch. I had done this so much that he had taken notice, and he questioned me about it. I never wanted my past to show up in any new relationship I found myself in, but it had, and Stan had taken notice. I didn't want to divulge the awful details of my abuse to him. I wanted to keep all of that behind me; however, the residual effects were still there and he was concerned. That's what I loved about him. He was observant. He asked me, why are you so jumpy when I try to kiss you? As I mentioned earlier I told him of my previous abusive relationships. He looked at me with such honesty and sincerity in his eyes and said, "I'll never do that to you." He also said a few choice words about the guys who had been abusive to me. Over time I began to relax. Eventually, the flinching subsided, and Stan never changed. He remained the man I took notice of, a person who genuinely cared for me, and he not only told me, but he also showed me.

After two years of Stan and I being involved, he called me as he had done every single night when he arrived home, even if he hadn't seen me that day. He would just call to say, "I'm home." It had gotten to the point where I could not fall asleep until he called. As we were about to say goodnight, he said, "I love you." I could not believe what I had just heard on the other end of the line. I was astonished by his statement and said to myself, *How could you say this and possibly mean it? You're married.* I was so taken by surprise that I couldn't and didn't know how to receive it, let alone respond to it, so I just stayed silent for what seemed like an eternity. He must have realized what he had said and my lack of a response that he probably regretted saying it. That was the first and last time he ever said those words. He began to show me, and that was good enough.

I thought that men who were involved with women outside of marriage couldn't catch feelings for that woman, and that it was all game if they expressed it as Stan had done. I thought it was ludicrous for him to say he loved me. I knew my place in that relationship with him, and I didn't have expectations because he was married. I didn't want to come between that any more than what I had done already, so I was staying in the safe zone. No feelings would get hurt because unrealistic expectations were assumed, so I was good and content. The more we grew closer, the more I was convicted of what I was doing. I struggled with it so much that I ended it, but we began again right where we left off. He knew I wanted to be in a serious monogamous relationship, and he could not give me that. Therefore, he never encouraged me to stay with him but was there regardless of my many breakups with him. I would pray to God, ask for forgiveness, but end right back where

I started. It was difficult for me to let go and let God. I had longed to be with a man who would love me and not use me as a punching bag and make me feel less than. Stan had come into my life and shown me all of these things I longed for, and he never changed so how could I let go so easily? It was not God's will for me to go through abuse over and over again, but He gives us free will and does not violate His word in doing so.

I was in a new kind of abuse, not physical but emotional. That man had come into my life and treated me with love and respect (at least that). He would say, "You make my marriage better." I didn't understand how or what he meant by that. He explained that when he was with me there were no issues, and when he was home, it was easier to deal with the stressors of home and family issues. I guess I was an outlet for him. I never got the chance to tell him over the six years we were involved how much he meant to me, but I'm sure he knew. I never told him that he taught me so much about how a man should treat me. I know you must be thinking, "How can you say that he taught you that, but he was cheating on his wife with you?" As crazy as it sounds, there are lessons to be taught and learned in life no matter the platform in which it occurs. Lessons take place in good and bad situations, and I had seen and had my share of bad. In my relationships, I have only known abuse. Now, seeing something totally different with Stan taught me the value of loving myself and that I am worthy of love, not abuse. He taught me that and more. He was the kind of person that you could easily be drawn to. He was easy to talk to and he was a great listener.

I remember when my parents met him for the first time on their first visit to New York. My dad talks about how nice he was to this very day. He was that kind of person. It's no wonder I loved him the way that I had. He made it easy for me to be me. He made it easy for me to smile. He made it easy for me to live and breathe again. I can go on and on about how he changed my life and brought me happiness I never imagined possible because all I knew was hurt and pain. No pain inflicted could ever hurt as deep as the pain I felt when hearing of Stan's tragic death.

In June of 2011, I got the news of my grandmother's passing (my Dad's mom). I had hoped to spend time with her after working summer school, but that chance never came to fruition. That was the second time I went home to Mississippi, one joyous and one sad occasion. I had gone down in May to see my son graduate high school and returned shortly afterwards. To get the call that my grandma had died, left me sad, so I made the decision that I would not work summer's again, and I would spend time with my family in Mississippi. I arrived for the funeral and planned to stay until school started in September, but plans did change. Back in May, my last conversation with Stan; it is one that I will never forget for the rest of my life. It was a warm and sunny day, and my phone rang. It was the voice I always loved to hear on the other end. He told me he couldn't talk earlier because he was home. That conversation led me to make a promise that he wouldn't have to worry about me calling him again. When I made a promise I aimed to keep it. Over the six-year span of our relationship, we had never ended our calls with goodbye, it was always, "I'll talk to you later, or I'll call you tomorrow." That time I said, "Goodbye." I didn't know that it would be goodbye forever.

I returned to New York a week later after attending my grandma's funeral due to an issue that needed to be addressed in my apartment. It was late June, and I was sticking to my promise I made to not call Stan. However, I was missing him, and he weighed heavy in my spirit. Instead of breaking my promise, I placed myself in the areas he frequented, in hopes of running into him, but there was no sign of him. I broke my promise and called his cell, which strangely went straight to voicemail. I became concerned, and I tried calling him from the payphone on the corner, no answer. I got his voicemail. I figured he'd see my calls and just return my call. It never happened.

On July 12, 2011, the reservoir on my car was punctured, and I need it installed. I went by one of Stan's friend's shops to have him install the device, but he wasn't at the shop when I arrived. He was just a few minutes away. Impatient me didn't want to wait, so I called Stan's other friend, the one he was closest to, just so I could find out how he was doing and if he's okay. He answered, and I told him the situation about my car. He said he would install the part for me.

Then, he quickly asked, "Did you hear what happened to Stan?"

I said, "No."

He said, "You didn't hear what happened to Stan?"

I replied again, "No."

I began to think that he was hurt from a motorcycle accident or something. I finally asked his friend, "What happened to him?"

He said, "Stan died."

Just like that, almost two months after my last and final conversation with the man that I loved, the one who showed me how I should be treated was gone. My body was numb, the beat of my heart was a loud thumping sound as if it was about to pump its last flow of blood away from what felt like my lifeless body. I got into my car somehow and manage to get to another friend of his to find out what happened and where his body was laid to rest. I arrived home but only by the grace of God because everything became a blur. I couldn't think, it hurt to breathe, and I wept in pain. My heart hurt. It was broken and saddened by the news. I retreated to my bed, and moments later I went to where he was laid to rest. I wept uncontrollably. I returned home to my bed and cried all day, all night. Days and weeks went by, and I continued to cry. *God, why?*

I understood why his spirit was so heavy on me for me to reach out to him. I believe it was him letting me know that he was no longer on this earth and that he would always be with me in my heart. I began to have dreams of him. In each dream, the colors he wore were significant. I took note and researched the meaning of them. In other dreams, he was protecting me as he had done in life. I had so many questions, and it seemed that I would not get answers. I began to grow closer to God. He heard my prayers and answered every question I had about Stan. I was talking to a friend and said, "I need closure, and I have so many questions."

She then said, "Melinda, you have to realize that those questions will never be answered."

Just as she spoke those words to me, the Lord said to me, "The reason you don't have closure is because his death is not final." After hearing that, I felt such a calm feeling sweep over me. I had peace and felt pain release its strong grip on my heart. I was fine for a few days after that revelation. I began talking to God more and finding comfort in spending time with Him. That was the first time that I'd ever heard the soft audible voice of God, and I crave more of it. I was at my lowest, and He revealed Himself to me. I became a believer and learned that He cared about me, and He knew the pain I was in. He wanted to heal me, and I wanted Him to take control and guide me through all that had happened. I wanted Him to reveal Himself more and more to me so that I could know Him for myself and not because of what I heard from someone else but because of the relationship I was cultivating with Him.

Reading His word became easy, and I yearned to hear from Him. I knew during this time that God was real and He was near, the breath in my lungs. He was my comforter. He heard my prayers. He answered every one of the questions I had. He cared about me. It's been fourteen years since that tragic day, yet I remember it like it was yesterday. The pain has softened over time, but the memories—and the happiness Stan brought into my life—still remain. And yes, I still miss him. Don't get me wrong—he showed me glimpses of love, moments that reminded me I *deserve* to be loved in all its many beautiful forms. But can I truly say he provided that kind of love? The answer is no.

Regardless of how well he treated me—and all the kind things he did that I had never seen in my previous relationships—the deeper issue remained: I had found myself caught in the very thing that caused my mother so much pain. It was the same pain our father's infidelity brought into our lives. I was now on the other side, doing the very thing I had once despised my daddy for. Adultery doesn't just break trust. It damages everyone it touches. Sometimes, the damage is just too deep to bounce back from easily. And in those vulnerable moments, the enemy creeps in—whispering lies that you deserve to stay with the person who broke you. All the while, he's stealing your time— time you should be spending with God, waiting for your Boaz. He's killing your well-being by keeping you emotionally entangled and destroying your ability to see yourself through God's eyes. But God says you are **fearfully and wonderfully made (Psalm 139:14, NIV).**

Stan's untimely death became a door to freedom. It wasn't easy to walk through— grief rarely is—but it marked a new beginning for me. And I've made a decision:

Satan will not be allowed to hold me hostage through deception, not as long as I keep my eyes on God and allow Him to love on me—fully, freely, and faithfully. Life has a funny way of rerouting you to the path you were meant to be on—especially when you finally decide to put God first. The truth is you can save yourself a whole lot of heartache and pain by letting Him lead from the start. But if you're anything like me and try to do it your own way, apart from Him, you may find yourself kissing a whole lot of frogs... and sometimes facing tragedy... before realizing that God was always meant to be the **Prince of your heart**—the one preparing you for your true king, your help meet, your partner for life. I'm grateful for the lessons. I'm grateful for the tests. They've shaped me into the woman I am today. While I still need God's guidance—always will—what I need most is for my relationship with Him to grow deeper, stronger, more intimate...day by day.

I understand now that my parents did the best that they could with what they knew and grew to know and understand in raising me and my siblings. I no longer hold on to the resentment and anger I held on to for many years towards my dad because of my upbringing. I finally got to ask my mom one final question on August 8, 2024, as she lay in her hospital bed in her bedroom under hospice care. I said, "Ma, did you feel that you couldn't take care of us if you had asked Daddy to leave?"

She responded in her tired voice, "Why are you asking me this?"

I said, "So I can add this to my book."

She responded once more, "That's in the past." So, I left it just as she had wanted, in the past. On August 11, 2024, my mom took her last breath as I sat at her side. The woman I know to be the strongest woman I have ever known. The woman who endured abuse and never said a mumbling word to her children but chose to deal with it in silence and with God. "Ma, I hope you are happy now that there is no more pain and sorrow to face here on earth. I love you always!"

8
Denzel: WHAT IF HE WAS THE ONE?

"You were supposed to have been wearing My last name."

I couldn't believe my eyes as I read the text message, *"You were supposed to have been wearing my last name."* My heart raced—an overwhelming mix of excitement at the thought of reconnecting and sadness for what could have been. I held back the emotions threatening to flood my mind and the tears welling up in my eyes. I sat in silence. No immediate response.

Nervously, I typed back, *"Oh really?"*

"I was in LOVE with you," came his reply. Denzel. My ex. My could have been husband. Only God knows.

Suddenly, the sound of my heart pounding in my chest became deafening. I wanted to stop texting, to ghost the man on the other side of the screen. *This can't be happening,* I thought—not after all these years. Twenty-eight years, to be exact. And yet, here it was—raw, unexpected, front and center. And I knew I had to see it through. I had to confront what I had buried deep inside me for so many years. I couldn't explain why, but something in my spirit knew—it was time. Time to have the conversation that had been avoided for far too long. And that time, I was ready to speak without hesitation.

The twenty-one-year-old young woman who had stepped into adulthood without any real guidance on life or love, who had learned her lessons the hard way, was finally prepared to face the twenty-three-year-old man she had once abandoned. We were both products of childhood trauma—wounded, yet drawn to each other—and ultimately torn apart by even more pain. And we were reconnecting after many years... through social media of all places. It was October 2021, and I had spent several months at my parents' home in Mississippi. Staying confined in my Brooklyn apartment during the pandemic had started to weigh heavily on me. I needed the freedom of going outside and breathing fresh air—without the constant worry of inhaling someone else's toxic virus. Being home in Mississippi brought a sense of peace. No cars constantly honking, no fire trucks blaring down the street, no noisy neighbors stomping overhead—just stillness. I could do absolutely nothing and still feel at ease. Despite the limitations that COVID-19 placed on one of the busiest cities in the world. There in Mississippi, life felt easier, slower, and far less taxing on the body and mind. During that visit, I found my happy place.

One Saturday afternoon, my sister and I decided to go out and do a bit of shopping in the city of Meridian. That simple outing took me right back down memory lane—to the time I met a young man named Denzel. Looking back to this time in my life, I was attending the local college there in my early twenties, newly determined to pursue higher education. My son was just two years old at the time, and I felt it was the perfect moment to get back into the field of nursing. I figured, why not return home to Mississippi and earn my degree like my sister had? It seemed like a good idea at the time to convince Ryan—the father of my child—to come along and be my support system. But what was I thinking? He had never supported me in anything, and deep down

I knew he probably never would. Still, that was my heart: always wanting to inspire others to do better for themselves. Unfortunately, that attempt at inspiration soon proved to be one very bad idea.

I had visited home plenty of times and made countless shopping trips to Meridian with my sister — it was just one of our rituals whenever I came down. But for some reason, the memories hit different during this particular visit in 2021. Maybe it was the crisp southern air, maybe it was the fact that I had finally learned to appreciate the silence of Mississippi over the sirens of Brooklyn. Whatever it was, something shifted. I remember seeing the sign pointing toward the Naval Base, and just like that—bam!—my mind went straight to my ex, and I couldn't help but smile.

I met Denzel while attending Meridian Community College, and to hear him tell the story, you'd think he had a surveillance camera and a narrator from a crime doc ready to play back our first encounter in vivid, 4K detail. Me? I couldn't recall the moment for the life of me—which, let's be honest, probably had a lot to do with the mental fog that came from years of emotional and physical abuse. Trauma has a way of erasing hard drives, you know? He said he walked over to me one Sunday afternoon as he was in the area hoping to find a church. He'd asked God to show him a church that would feed his soul. He had driven past a few, but none of them moved him. Still, he kept getting a feeling that one was in the area of my location. He stopped and asked some locals who were at a McDonald's, and somehow, he ended up at the campus across the street—at my dormitory.

He recalled walking past other young ladies as we were just standing outside, and he stepped right up to me. I don't know what he said, but I do remember saying to myself, *Why is he coming towards me when other girls are standing here who are better looking and don't have the responsibility of caring for a child?* But he stepped right up to me and said whatever he said, and I responded with, "I have a child," and looked him dead in the face to see his reaction. He said, "That doesn't matter." I thought it was important information for a man to know before he even thought about trying to establish a relationship with me. He said he liked my shyness and innocence, and when I smiled, that was the ticket. I was quite the shy one back then, and I still carried an innocence about me because I was still learning about the world and the people around me. I was trusting and accepted what was told to me—until proven otherwise. By this time, my relationship with Ryan had taken yet another turn in the wrong direction, and I had finally had enough of his abuse. He stopped by my dormitory one night and started an argument with me about—God knows what. Truthfully, he was the last thing on my mind. I was now involved with someone who treated me kindly, someone who was slowly becoming a part of my life—and I wanted him to be.

During that heated altercation, Ryan pushed me down onto the pavement, and I ended up hurting my wrist. Then, he just walked away, right back across the street to the dormitory where he was staying. I went back into my room, and one of my dormmates immediately noticed I was hurt—maybe she saw the tears in my eyes or just the look on my face. She demanded that I call the police and report it. I was hesitant at first, but then I decided to do it— because I was ready. Ready for that chapter of my life with him to be over. The police arrived, took my statement, and asked if I needed to go to the emergency room. Then, they went across the street, and by the next day, Ryan had been arrested. I felt a wave of relief wash over me. I hoped this would finally teach him that he couldn't go on thinking he owned me or had the right to control me. It was time someone told him—through action, not words— that he couldn't get away with what he'd done.

For the first time in a long time, I breathed a sigh of relief. I felt empowered. I had the upper hand, and I was moving on. But one heated argument would prove me wrong—and set me on a course that would change my life forever. I was really enjoying the direction my love life was taking for once. I had met Denzel, who actually seemed to be genuinely interested in me—no red flags, no side eyes, just real, solid interest. He would come to campus just to see me. When I visited my parents on the weekends, he'd drive forty-eight miles (give or take a few backroads and deer crossings) to visit me out in what we affectionately call "the sticks." And trust me, it was *not* Meridian. We're talking straight-up country—pitch-black roads at night with more curves than a soap opera and just as much drama if you weren't careful. One wrong turn and you'd find yourself in a ditch, or worse, rolling down a gully. But even with no GPS and zero familiarity with the backwoods of Mississippi, when I invited him, he found his way—no hesitation. And that was major in my book. If a man was willing to come *all the way out there*, he had to be serious—and Denzel? Oh, he was clocking miles like a man on a mission. I absolutely loved when he'd show up unexpectedly. That made me feel special, like I had a secret admirer who was actually mine. I was soaking up every minute we spent together. He showed me something totally different— respect, kindness, consistency—and I started to picture us as more than just "boyfriend and girlfriend." Dare I say... long-term potential. Sometimes it honestly felt too good to be true. I mean, there was this handsome guy actually *choosing* me? Little ol' me? Let's not forget, I had my fair share of self-esteem issues. Not because people told me I was unattractive, but because emotional abuse messes with your head in a way that mirrors rejection. My son's father never invited me anywhere—didn't matter if he was just going to sit in the park or post up in front of the building. I stayed home. Every. Single. Time. So yeah, being chosen, pursued, and valued felt like brand-new territory.

I remember having a conversation with one of my closest friends one day, and somehow we slid right into the topic of our exes—you know, the ones that make you wonder if you were under some kind of spell. She looked at me and said, "I don't know what you saw in him—he wasn't even cute!" And I couldn't help but laugh because I had heard that line more times than I could count. Truth is, it was never about the looks. There was just *something* about him that pulled me in. It wasn't the face—it was the charm. That Gemini charm that could talk a nun out of her vows. And me? I fell for it like a fly on a sticky trap. Or better yet, like maggots on rotten meat—gross, but accurate. I was not into all that astrological stuff, but for some reason, most of my relationships involved men born under the Gemini sign. My first experience was my dad. I watched that man like a hawk—his mood swings were something out of a soap opera: Dr. Jekyll and Mr. Hyde had nothing on him. On payday, he'd come home looking like he was ready to fight the air—just so nobody would dare ask him for money. And when my sister and I hit that courting stage and wanted to go to the movies with the boys we liked, he shut that down real quick with a firm "absolutely not." But I'll tell you what—I lived for the weekends. That was my chance to catch the good side of Daddy. He'd usually get a little tipsy and that's when the money would *sometimes* start flowing... but only if we asked. Don't expect him to just hand it over—nope, we had to put in a full application and hope it got approved by drunk Dad.

The second Gemini to stroll into my life was a classmates' cousin. Yep, another one. And let me tell you, the Gemini traits were all there—loved the ladies, smooth talker, full of charm—and there I was, head over heels like I hadn't seen this movie before starring my own father. My third Gemini was Ryan (insert dramatic sigh here). Then came number four—Denzel. I guess I will never know what the outcome would have been. And last, but certainly not least, number five was Marcus. Lord knows I should've known better with him, but nope—I signed up anyway like I was enrolling in Gemini University. So, you see, I'd done my time with men born under that sign. And now? When a guy so much as compliments my shoes, my first question isn't "What's your name?" It's "What's your sign?" Because if he says Gemini, I know I've already survived that course—and I'm not repeating the class.

So, then came this Navy guy—all charming, and might I add (again) handsome—sneaking up on me like a plot twist I didn't see coming. The more time we spent together, the more I felt myself slipping out of the emotional chokehold of my past abuser. It was like therapy, but cuter. I was opening up to someone who was the complete opposite of what I was used to—gentle, attentive, and didn't treat me like I came with a user manual he refused to read. But I'll be honest, in the back of my mind I was on Gemini Watch, just waiting for those signature personality shifts to creep in like an unwelcome sequel. But surprise—nothing. Not even a flicker. It was like I had finally met a man who didn't come with an expiration date or a warning label. I started to feel something I hadn't felt in a long time—peace. Real, no-side-eye-needed, put-your-guard-down peace. He didn't raise his voice, didn't question my every move, and wasn't trying to compete with my toddler for attention. I found myself laughing more, sleeping better, and even thinking, *maybe all men aren't emotionally unavailable aliens sent here to test our patience.* It was wild. For once, I wasn't playing emotional dodgeball—I was actually in something that felt... easy. And let me tell you, when you've been surviving chaos for so long, *ease* feels like a red flag until you realize, no sis—that's just what healthy feels like.

Denzel and I were both young when we crossed paths—he was twenty-three, I was twenty-one, and we were just figuring life out one decision at a time. He had just joined the Navy and was stationed in Meridian for a few months before our stars aligned. For the first time in a while, I felt like my life was heading in the right direction. We were genuinely happy with each other, and it felt like we wanted to see just how far this thing could go. We never sat down and mapped out our five-year plan—nah, we just moved with the flow. And honestly, the flow was smooth, easy, and for once, drama-free. It was like cruising down a back road with the windows down and the radio up—no traffic, no potholes, just good vibes and possibility. After we reconnected on social media, he told me that he had cut off all other prospects before our second date. I remember asking him, "How could you have known that early on that I was the one you wanted to date exclusively?"

His response, "I didn't want to risk losing you."

On that day, my sister and I went shopping, and seeing the sign for the Navy Base, my mind went straight to Denzel. For some strange reason I still can't explain, I could not get him out of my head—no matter what I did, he kept showing up in my thoughts almost every single day. A week went by, and he was still lingering there, front and center. My spirit just wouldn't rest until I searched for him on social media.

As I was walking through my parents' house, it hit me again—this time stronger than before. I knew I couldn't shake it, so I gave in and did what I felt I was being led to do. I opened up Messenger, typed in his full government name, and boom—there he was. Different, yes, but somehow even more handsome as an older gentleman. Reluctantly, I typed: *I'm not sure if you're the right person, but were you ever stationed in Meridian, MS?"* Then, I waited for him to respond. When I didn't get a response right away, I felt rejected—in some weird, unnecessary kind of way. I started talking to myself like, *"He's mad at you for leaving him the way you did."* Honestly, I couldn't blame him if he was. I had to own that. I was partly responsible for our relationship ending the way it did—just when things were hitting a pivotal moment. But at that time, I felt like I had no other choice. And let's be real—choosing between the lesser of two evils is still choosing evil. No matter how you flip it, spin it, or sugarcoat it, it's still a hard pill to swallow. And I, and only I, had to pick one and live with whatever came next.

I had searched for Denzel a few times after we separated—twenty-eight years ago. Back then, there was no such thing as social media, just handwritten letters and landlines. I remember calling him a few weeks after I left, just to hear his voice. He sounded broken, and I could tell there were still so many unanswered questions. We talked, but only around the edges of what really needed to be said. We tried to make sense of it all—to fix something that had already fallen apart. His suggestions for how to handle my situation didn't feel rational to me at the time, and I made decisions fueled by emotion, frustration, and confusion. I was angry, I was torn, and I was unsure—and that's never a good place to be when you're making choices that affect someone else's heart.

It was 1992, and summer break was right around the corner. Students were packing up and heading home to finally get a break after a long semester of studying. I was back at my parents' house, and honestly, I was just happy to be spending every day with my son again. He was growing up so beautifully, and I had missed him deeply while living on campus. Life at home was going as well as it could, all things considered—but my dad and I still weren't seeing eye to eye, even with me now being a young mother. I hated having to stay under his roof with my child, and I went out of my way to keep my son out of his path as much as possible. I knew my father cared for my son and didn't think he'd ever treat him the way he treated me and my siblings growing up. But all of that changed—and boy, was I wrong.

Something happened one evening that involved him yelling at my baby, and it led to a heated altercation between us. The details of that night are a bit blurry now—it was so long ago—but I do know this: nothing would have made me leave so abruptly unless it involved my child. I had found ways to tolerate living under the same roof with my father, and I had Denzel, who would visit when he had time off and whisk me away from the madness. He was my escape from it all. I vaguely remember my dad raising his hand and hitting me after I told him not to speak to my child the way he had. Without hesitation, I scooped up my son and walked down the dark country road to my uncle's house. I called the only person I knew would protect me—the only one I had to call—and that was Denzel. As always, he showed up and rescued me from the madness. I recall him coming to my parents' house, and just as we were getting ready to leave, my dad pulled out a pistol and fired a shot into the ceiling. Now, I wasn't scared—one thing I've learned about Gemini men is that they're mostly bark and very little bite. Denzel, my son, and I got in the car and rode back to Meridian, where we stayed in a hotel for the night. I was broken and confused at this point. My mind was racing—thought after thought pounding in my head. *Where am I gonna go now? How do I fix this? God, what am I gonna do?* One thing I knew for sure: I was not going back to my parents' house.

After telling Denzel everything that had happened, I let him know I couldn't return there, and that I had made the decision to go back to the one place I had hoped to avoid—New York. Denzel suggested taking my son and me to Louisiana to stay with his mother until he could get an apartment for us. But I didn't think that was a good idea. I didn't know her—or anyone in his family, for that matter—and I wasn't comfortable being in a place where I didn't know a single soul. So, I made up my mind: I was going back to New York. It hurt to say that to Denzel, especially as he pleaded with me not to go, but I was adamant. I needed to leave Mississippi once and for all—away from the family that was supposed to protect me, but instead had become the source of so much hurt and pain.   He said, "If you go back, he's gonna start beating you again." Deep down, I knew he was right. But I was scared, not thinking clearly—emotionally drained—and my son was at the center of it all. How was I supposed to protect both of us from abuse coming at me from both ends? My dad and his father—both abusers. I made my choice, and I've lived with it every single day since. It's a regret that still lingers. Denzel was left behind. I stepped back into a life filled with years of abuse—years that carved a scar so deep into my heart, soul, and spirit that only God could heal it. That's the consequence of not seeking God first and trusting His plans for your life.

Looking back now, I understand that God was trying to offer me a lifeline, and I ignored it out of fear, confusion, and emotional exhaustion. I thought I was making the responsible choice, the safe choice—but in reality, I was just choosing the pain I already knew over the unknown that could have brought peace. It took me years, bruises both seen and unseen, and tear-soaked prayers to finally realize that survival isn't the same as living. And while I can't change the past, I've learned that healing begins when you stop running from the truth and start walking with God, even if you're limping at first.   I often wondered what would have happened had I stayed in Mississippi, taken that chance, and allowed someone who truly cared for me to love me through the pain. But I wasn't ready. Not then. I was still operating from wounds, not wisdom.

Still, even in my darkest moments, I now see that God never left me. He was always there—quietly, patiently, waiting for me to surrender. And slowly, with each broken piece I handed over, He began to rebuild me. The scars remain, yes, but they no longer define me. They are reminders of where I've been and Who brought me through. Maybe that chapter of my life didn't end the way I wanted, but it taught me something deeper than any fairytale ending could: that redemption is real, and healing is possible—even if it comes years later, in the quiet moments when you finally realize your worth isn't tied to your pain, but to the God who loves you through it.

Now, back to October 2021. Denzel responded to my message. I was like a kid in a candy store when I saw his reply the next day. At first, he played it cool—acting like he didn't quite remember who I was. But then he started reminiscing, trying to recall the last time he'd seen or heard from me. His timeline was way off, but honestly, that didn't matter. What mattered was that he remembered me. And just like that, we were both on a trip down memory lane. I didn't know what I was expecting. A polite hello? A memory shared and then silence? But the moment I saw his words, it all came rushing back —

the way he used to look at me like I mattered, like I wasn't invisible. He remembered things I had forgotten, things I thought pain had erased. He told me I was supposed to have worn his last name. I stared at the message, stunned, caught somewhere between grief and giddy disbelief. How do you respond to something like that when your life has taken every turn but the one that led back to him? I confessed that he had been right all along—his prediction that I'd be abused again by my son's father had come true. Life for me had been nothing short of hell. He said it was the same for him — that he had tried looking for me a few times. He told me he'd even come back to Meridian for work on the base and had tried to find me but couldn't remember how to get to my parents' house. I told him that I had looked for him too and eventually found him on Facebook. I mentioned the picture he had posted of himself with his family and how I didn't reach out back then because it looked like he had moved on and built a life. I didn't want to intrude. He told me he had forgotten to update his profile picture, but he was no longer married. From there, we went on and on, catching up on everything that had happened in our lives since we parted ways.

Some of the things he shared broke my heart—and I know they'll stay with me for the rest of my life. I told him that, at the time, I felt like I had no other choice. He told me he had been in love with me and had wanted to marry me. I loved him too. I felt safe with him. Even now, I question the decision I made to walk away, to leave him behind. I can't help but wonder how different my life might have been if I had stayed. But this... this is the regret I live with. I chose survival, not knowing it would cost me something just as valuable— love, a family of my own and a bright future. Not just any love, but the kind that didn't ask me to earn it. I left, thinking I was protecting myself, but some nights, I wonder if I was also running from the one person who truly saw me. Seeing his name pop up on my screen felt like a knock on a door I'd long boarded up.

When he said he never stopped looking for me, something inside me cracked open. Time may have passed, but some connections aren't erased by years—they just lie dormant, waiting. I assumed that was what the constant promptings to reach out to him was about, to finally close that chapter in this journey of healing. Still, I know this: Denzel gave me a glimpse of what love could look like when it's not built on fear or control. He didn't come to rescue me. He simply reminded me I was worth rescuing. Although life has taken us both on different journeys hoping that we would hopefully pick up the pieces where we left off, but time has run its course and we must make the most of what God has truly given us, the freedom of choice. I choose life. I choose to spend it with of course my maker, my Heavenly Father, myself, my children and my family and those that are connected to me. I'm learning to seek God first and trust that His plans are far greater than any plan I could ever imagine for myself and I am grateful for the process and the lessons that come in growing in the knowledge of my creator.

So, to you Denzel. Thank you for your love and protection when I needed it but didn't comprehend it and for all the darkness and pain that shrouded my spiritual and physical sight. I'm sorry for the pain I caused you, and I believe I was supposed to have your last name.

📖
✦ Key Takeaways:
When Love Finds Its Way Back ✦

- Love leaves fingerprints on the soul. Some connections are timeless, echoing even after years of silence.

- God's timing is perfect. When we let go, we allow Him to move in ways we never expected.

- Reconnection brings healing. A single message can open doors to conversations that were buried but never forgotten.

- There is power in being honest with yourself. Revisiting the past takes courage, but it also frees you.

- You are still lovable — even after the storm. Love can recognize you, even with your scars.

- Regret can teach, not torment. You are not your past. You are what you do with it now.

♀ Reader Reflection Prompt

- Is there someone or something from your past you've never fully released – or forgiven?

- What truths have you been afraid to say out loud, even to yourself?

- How would it feel to tell your story honestly – not for them, but for your own healing?

- Where might God be nudging you to revisit or release something you thought was over.

Write a letter you'll never send. Or maybe you will.

Now that I've learned—and am still learning—through life's many experiences, I can finally continue in the healing process. I'm finding closure and receiving the kind of healing that only comes from confronting the trauma that once broke me, but ultimately shaped me for the better. I forgive—because in forgiving, I reclaim my smile, my joy, and my peace. I understand now that my parents did the best that they could with what they knew and grew to know and understand in raising me and my siblings. I no longer hold on to the resentment and anger I held on to for many years towards my dad because of my upbringing.

Part Two

AFTERWORD
A Letter to My Dad

Dear Daddy,

It's taken me many years to finally put this into words. I carried so much anger for so long—anger about how you treated Mom, me, and my siblings. But this letter isn't about anyone else's story; it's about mine. I want you to know that I forgive you. I believe you did the best you knew how to do when it came to raising me. It wasn't the best, and it wasn't easy, but it was what you knew. I can't hold that against you anymore. What I can say is that I learned from it. I made it my mission not to repeat those same patterns with my own children. And while I wasn't perfect, I think I did alright—I raised them with what I knew, and they've grown into good young adults.

You don't know how much I needed you to be there for me to protect me when I became a doormat to my children's father to just step all over me and disregard me and the boys. He treated me like trash to be trampled on. I needed you there to teach me how to defend myself in situations like those that arose in my life. I needed you to tell me which boy/man was good for me and teach me to walk away from those that were not good for me. I needed you more than you will ever know. I endured more heartaches and heartbreaks than I could remember, and I always wanted to run and tell you so that you would protect your second-born daughter.

I held all of this in for a long time, but at the end of me finishing this book, I felt the nudging from God to write this letter to you. As He would have it, He knew that it was time for the healing process to begin. It can only begin when true forgiveness is enacted.

Daddy, I love you and I forgive you a thousand times over.

Love,
Linda

ACKNOWLEDGEMENTS

There would be no me without my mother, Mrs. Brenda Ann Jones. She's the woman who raised me and my siblings the best way she knew how—with love, a sharp side-eye, and the occasional well-deserved whipping when we stepped too far out of line. Not that we were bad kids. I don't believe children are *bad*—they just like to test the waters, stretch the boundaries, and see if they'll snap back. And sometimes, those stretched lines led straight to consequences...the kind that had me running in frantic zigzags, trying to escape my mama and that switch she used to express her very... *passionate* form of love.

My mom was a woman who held a lot inside. She never really said how she felt—at least not to me or my siblings—especially when something truly affected her. Back when we were all still living at home, she kept those emotions tucked away, wrapped in silence. Now, even as an adult looking back, I realize...I still don't remember her ever really speaking those feelings out loud.

As she neared her departure from this world, my mother never spoke a word about her life as a wife. Even in the thick of her battle with cancer, if you asked, *"How are you feeling?"* she'd answer softly, *"I'm alright."* And I believed her. Not just because she said it, but because she truly wasn't in physical pain. She told me God had promised to take care of her—and He did.

I believe He spared her the pain of suffering because she had already carried so much in her life. She had endured enough. So, when it was time, He made sure she left this world pain-free, gently preparing her to come home to Him—to a place where pain and suffering no longer exist. My mom is deeply missed. And I will always remember the smile she wore— even when it was hiding a pain she never spoke of. I admire her for her grace, her quiet strength, her relentless fight, and her unwavering reverence for God.

"Mom, I watched you take your final breath. You slipped peacefully from this world and into the presence of God. While you're no longer here physically, I know I'll see you again.

You're never truly far from us—we carry you in our hearts every single day. If you were here, I'd sit beside you and read these pages of my completed work. You'd probably laugh, deny half of it, and turn your mouth up the way you always did when Teresa and I would start recounting childhood memories—especially the ones under your roof with Daddy. No matter what I've written in these pages, I know this: God placed me with you. And God doesn't make mistakes. Thank you for loving us the best way you knew how. We'll honor your dying wish, and I hope—more than anything—that you're smiling from Heaven... proud of what you see."

To my sister, Teresa, who was there pushing me to write, write, write. I took your advice, and I wrote at all hours of the night and into the early morning hours while you were sleeping. You have been my BIGGEST cheerleader, and I have enjoyed having you as my very first reader. Thank you for the laughter as I read the pages of this book to you. It has been a bittersweet road down memory lane with you by my side, laughing and crying all the way. Thank you again.

To my classmate, L.N., who I saw for the first time since graduating high school at church on Dec. 24, 2023. You prophesied to me and said, "Write that book, it's going to be healing for you and your family." I never told you that I was writing a book about my life. But GOD! You have since transitioned from this life to be with the Lord. I will always remember our very short reunion and your words of kindness. I am so sorry for not calling you when God placed you in my spirit to call and talk to you.

To Prophetess, Tysha, who God allowed her to be His mouthpiece and tell me to "Write that book." But God!

To my three sons, we have been through a lot and many things I tried to shield you from still found its way in, but by the grace of God, He was there always protecting you all. I tried to be the mother I needed to be to the gifts He gave me, to love, care for, and nurture into the young men that you have become today. Thank you for believing in me when I didn't believe in myself. Thank you for wiping away the tears that I often tried to hide and the hugs that warmed my heart and mended the often-broken pieces. I LOVE YOU! Always.

I want to thank the gospel group Mary Mary for their song "Forgiven Me." This song and God's word got me through the tough times.

Women in Dysfunctional Relationships

Yes, research shows that women who repeatedly find themselves in dysfunctional relationships often have underlying psychological and relational patterns rooted in early attachment experiences, including dysfunctional relationships with their fathers or other primary caregivers. Here's a breakdown of the factors that contribute to this cycle:

1. Attachment Theory & Early Childhood Relationships

• According to **attachment theory** (Bowlby, 1969), the way we relate to caregivers in early childhood significantly impacts our adult relationships. If a woman's relationship with her father (or another primary caregiver) was **inconsistent, neglectful, critical, or abusive**, she may develop an **insecure attachment style** (anxious, avoidant, or fearful-avoidant), making dysfunctional relationships feel familiar and even subconsciously "safe."

• A **father's absence (emotional or physical)** can lead to an internalized sense of unworthiness, causing some women to seek validation in romantic partners.

2. Parental Modeling & Normalization of Dysfunction

- If a woman **witnessed** dysfunctional parental relationships growing up, she may unconsciously **normalize** behaviors such as emotional unavailability, verbal abuse, manipulation, or neglect.

- **Social learning theory** (Bandura, 1977) suggests that children model the behaviors they observe. If a father was **controlling, emotionally detached, or abusive**, a woman might unconsciously be drawn to partners who exhibit similar traits, even when they cause distress.

3. Trauma Bonds & The "Familiar Pain" Dynamic

- Trauma bonding (Carnes, 1997) explains why some women feel deeply attached to unhealthy partners despite experiencing harm. If a father figure created a **cycle of love and rejection**, a woman may develop **hyper-vigilance in relationships**, confusing intermittent affection with real love.

- The **"familiar pain"** dynamic means that a woman may seek **unconscious reenactment** of childhood wounds in an attempt to gain mastery over them.

4. Low Self-Worth & Core Beliefs

- Negative core beliefs such as "I am not enough" or "I have to earn love" often stem from childhood experiences where love felt **conditional, inconsistent, or withheld**.

- This can lead to **codependency**, where a woman over-invests in unhealthy relationships, trying to "fix" a partner or prove her worth through self-sacrifice.

5. Fear of Abandonment & Emotional Dependency

- If a father was **emotionally or physically unavailable**, a woman may develop a **deep fear of abandonment**, making it difficult to leave even toxic relationships.

- This is common in **anxious-preoccupied attachment styles**, where a woman may **cling to unhealthy partners** out of fear of being alone.

6. Cultural & Societal Conditioning

- Women are often socialized to be **nurturers and caretakers**, leading some to **stay in dysfunctional relationships** believing they can change or "save" their partner.

- Religious or cultural beliefs about **marriage, submission, or suffering in silence** may also play a role in staying in unhealthy dynamics.

Breaking the Cycle: Therapeutic Interventions

- **Attachment-based therapy** can help women recognize patterns from childhood and heal insecure attachment wounds.

- **Cognitive Behavioral Therapy (CBT)** can help identify and shift negative core beliefs about self-worth and relationships.

- **Inner child work & re-parenting** techniques help women learn how to give themselves the emotional security they lacked in childhood.

- **Boundary setting & self-empowerment coaching** teach women to recognize red flags and establish healthier relationship patterns.

Dear Daughters,

Yes—you.

The one holding this book, wondering if your story matters.

The one whose been strong for so long, you're not sure how to be anything else. The ont who still wrestles with the words.

"Am I enough?"

Let me tell you something I wish someone had told me a long time ago:

You are more than what happened to you.

You are more than your mistakes.

More than the silence, the scars, the unansweed pravers, or the "Why me?" You are worthy of love, right now exactly as you are.

This book isn't written from a place of perfection. I'm still healing, still learning, still talking to God about things I don't fully understand. But I've come far enough to turn around, look you in the eye through these pages and say,

You're not alone.

You don't have to hrink to fit someone else's comfort. You don't have to keep carrying to make others feel better,

Your yoice matters.

Your feelings matter.

Melinda

And your healing is not a burden—it's a birthright.

RESOURCES

Understanding the Roots of Dysfunctional Relationships

This resource provides research-backed links and summaries on how early family dynamics—especially parental and father-daughter relationships—can shape how women experience and choose romantic relationships in adulthood. It also includes faith-based resources for encouragement and healing.

1. Attachment Theory & Relationships

Attachment theory (developed by John Bowlby and Mary Ainsworth) explains how early bonds with caregivers affect future romantic relationships.

- Psychology Today - Attachment Theory Overview:
  https://www.psychologytoday.com/us/basics/attachment-theory

- Psychological Bulletin (2019) Meta-Analysis:
  https://doi.org/10.1037/bul0000221

2. Father-Daughter Relationships & Adult Romantic Patterns

Research shows a daughter's relationship with her father impacts her self-esteem and relationship choices.

- Fatherly - How Dads Shape Daughters' Relationships:
  https://www.fatherly.com/love-money/how-fathers-influence-daughters-relationships

- Child & Adolescent Social Work Journal Study: https://doi.org/10.1080/02739615.2010.503043

3. Parental Modeling of Relationships

Children often repeat relationship behaviors they saw growing up—healthy or not.

- Psych Central - Why We Choose Dysfunctional Relationships: https://psychcentral.com/lib/why-we-choose-dysfunctional-relationships

- Social Learning Theory Overview: https://www.simplypsychology.org/bandura.html

4. Trauma Bonding & Familiar Pain

Trauma bonding occurs when emotional highs and lows in unhealthy relationships create addictive attachment.

- Medical News Today - What Is Trauma Bonding?: https://www.medicalnewstoday.com/articles/trauma-bonding

- National Domestic Violence Hotline - Trauma Bonds: https://www.thehotline.org/resources/why-do-people-stay-in-abusive-relationships-trauma-bonds/

5. Faith-Based Encouragement for Parents & Teens

Faith-based insights can guide teens and parents in cultivating healthier relationship models.

- Focus on the Family - How Your Marriage Affects Your Kids: https://www.focusonthefamily.com/parenting/how-your-marriage-affects-your-kids/

- Bible.com Devotional - Choosing the Right Friends: https://www.bible.com/reading-plans/10710-choosing-the-right-friends

ABOUT THE AUTHOR

Melinda Jones realized that the secret to figuring out who she is—and how she got here—was to rewind the tape and go back to where it all started. The people, places, and questionable life choices that shaped her as a kid, a teenager (yikes), and eventually the adult she is today all played their part. This book is about those beginnings. Most importantly, it is about the impact of Melinda's relationship with her parents—especially her dad (brace yourself). Like many girls her age, she once dreamed of marriage, kids, and the whole white-picket-fence fantasy. But not every girl dreams of a happily ever after. Some just dream of getting the heck out!

Just when she thought she was finally making her grand escape, her childhood experiences came sprinting after her like a horror movie's villain who just wouldn't die. The nightmare didn't vanish—it just got a makeover. She mistook pain for love, finding herself drawn to men who were just as wounded as her. Their internal scars became her physical ones, and for far too long, she believed that was just how life worked. But then—plot twist—God showed up, swung open the escape hatch, and shoved her toward the exit door. Of course, in true dramatic fashion, that healing process came with its own surprise—a mix of beauty, tragedy, and her overall healing.

MELINDA JONES is an educator, a school counselor, a single mom to three amazing sons, and now—officially—a first-time author. Her passion is working with children of all age groups teaching various subjects. In her spare time, she enjoys spending time with family in her childhood hometown in Mississippi. When she's not juggling work and helping others, she's out enjoying the fast-paced energy of New York City, where she has resided for the past thirty-six years.